Word Recognition for Listeners

PronPack

PRONUNCIATION FOR LISTENING

Mark Hancock

HANCOCK McDONALD ELT

Other books in the PronPack collection are:

PronPack 1: Pronunciation workouts
Extended choral drill activities.

PronPack 2: Pronunciation Puzzles
Puzzles and game-like activities.

PronPack 3: Pronunciation Pairworks
Communicative practice activities.

PronPack 4: Pronunciation Poems
Poems, raps and chants to highlight various pronunciation points.

PronPack 5: Pronunciation of English for Spanish Speakers
Activities for working on the kinds of difficulties experienced by Spanish-speaking learners.

PronPack 6: Pronunciation of English for Brazilian Learners
Activities for working on the kinds of difficulties experienced by learners whose first language is Brazilian Portuguese.

PronPack: Connected Speech for Listeners
Ideas and activities for raising awareness of connected speech.

PronPack:
Word Recognition for Listeners

Mark Hancock

Hancock McDonald
ENGLISH LANGUAGE TEACHING
Published by Hancock McDonald ELT
Chester. CH1 2AW UK
www.hancockmcdonald.com

First Published 2023

ISBN: 9781838404048

Author: Mark Hancock
Consultant and Editor: Annie McDonald
Design: Amanda Hancock
Graphics: Heliographic
Illustration: Mark Hancock
Audio: Mark Hancock

PronPack Books www.pronpack.com

Contents

PronPack: Word Recognition for Listeners

Contents 4

Pronunciation for Listening 6

Introduction 7

Section A Practical tips 11

A1 Teach Spoken Word Recognition 12

A2 Break the spell of the written form 14

A3 Show how words are simplified in speech 16

A4 Prepare learners for word variability 19

A5 Highlight the structure of syllables 22

A6 Know how to divide words into syllables 24

A7 Pay attention to word stress 26

A8 Highlight stress patterns and variation 28

A9 Raise awareness of weak syllables 30

A10 Raise the awareness of rhythm 32

A11 Help learners to spot word boundaries 34

A12 Encourage active listening 36

Section B Word recognition games 39

B1 Open syllable maze 40

B2 Cluster maps 42

B3 Land of lost letters 44

B4 Syllable Tennis 46

B5 Flipping Syllables 49

B6 Crossverbs puzzle 51

B7 Schwa Riddles 53

B8 Stepping Stones 55

B9 Syllable Soup 57

B10 Syllable Spotting 58

B11 Lost Middles Maze 60

B12 Trictation 62

Section C Lexis for listeners 65

C1 Word endings *er, or, ar, our, re* 66
C2 Word ending *ate* 68
C3 Word endings *ory, ary* and *ery* 71
C4 Word endings *ic* and *ical* 73
C5 Word endings *ant, ent, ance* and *ence* 75
C6 Verb Beginnings *a, co, su* 77
C7 Verb Beginnings *be, de, re, pre* 79
C8 Verb Beginnings *con, en, in* 82
C9 Noun ending *ity* 84
C10 Nouns ending *ation* 87
C11 Noun endings *ion* and *ian* 90
C12 Noun ending *ture* 92
C13 Adjectives ending *able* and *ible* 95
C14 Adjective endings *ious* and *ous* 97
C15 Adjective endings *al* and *ile* 99
C16 Noun endings like *ology* and *onomy* 101
C17 Adverb ending *ly* 103
C18 Place name endings like *ton* and *ham* 105

Section D Resources 107

D1 PronPack Sound Chart 108
D2 Glossary of Terms 109
D3 Bibliography 113
D4 About the Author 114
D5 Acknowledgements 115
D6 About PronPack 116

Pronunciation for Listening

Pronunciation is all about speaking clearly, right? Wrong! It's also about listening fluently.

You have probably heard learners saying things like, '*I've studied English for years and I can understand perfectly in class, but out in the real world I understand nothing!*'. So what is going wrong? What is missing in our lessons? How can we help learners deal with authentic spoken English? I think the answer is we need to focus more on pronunciation for listening.

That is the idea behind the series **PronPack: Pronunciation for Listening**. The books combine practical tips for focusing on the spoken language with classroom materials specifically designed for this purpose. They are innovative but at the same time, very reader-friendly and easy to use. The first book in the series focuses on spoken English as it relates to grammar, and the second as it relates to vocabulary.

At the *grammatical* level, **Connected Speech for Listeners** looks at the way words, especially short grammatical words like articles and pronouns, blend together in context. These words may be simple, but they are often difficult for the listener to hear in connected speech.

At the *lexical* level, **Word Recogniton for Listeners** focuses on the way longer words vary and change in spoken English. Your learner may understand words such as *comfortable* or *secretary* perfectly well while reading, but find them hard to recognise in spoken English

Introduction

This book is designed to help teachers of English understand what is involved in a key listening skill: recognising words in speech. It also provides ideas and materials for use in class.

Spoken word recognition

Unlike the written word, the spoken word is different every time you hear it – think of all the different voices and accents in the world. How do listeners ever recognise these various versions as being the same word? This crucial aspect of the listening skill is known as 'spoken word recognition', and that is what this book is about. Various factors influence a learner's ability to achieve word recognition.

The influence of spelling

Written forms of words tend to stick in the memory more strongly than the spoken forms. Unfortunately, in English, the written form is often misleading and often leads to mispronunciation. For example, many learners pronounce *comfortable* like *come for table*. This also leads to listening difficulties: if the learner expects words to sound like their written form, they may not recognise them in speech. .

The influence of variation

When we hear a word, we compare it to words which are stored in our memory and look for a match. However, words don't have only one form. Consider a word such as *actually*. If you're speaking really carefully, this may have four syllables, but said quickly it may come out as only two, like *ashley*. To help learners build up their repertoire of stored versions of a word, we need to expose them to more variety.

The influence of first language

Listeners do not hear neutrally. We are primed to pay attention to features which are important in our language, while ignoring features which are not. For example, if word stress is important in your first language, you tend to notice it; if it is not, then you tend to be 'stress deaf'. With our learners, we somehow need to prime them to pay attention to features which may not be common in their L1, but which are common in English.

The influence of memory

Listeners have to process what they're hearing in real time. This means making guesses as you listen and then checking and revising your guesses as you go along. For example, to begin with, a sentence may sound like *It's a fish*, but as you continue to listen you realise the actual sentence was *It's official*. This makes demands on your working memory – you have to be able to hold the first version in mind long enough to revise it to the second version. Learners often struggle with this.

This book and how to use it

The main body of this book consists of three sections. **Section A** is background reading. **Sections B** and **C** contain practical teaching ideas and materials.

Section A

Section A contains 12 practical tips with advice and suggestions about how to teach word recognition for listening. You can read this section straight through for a complete overview of the issues involved. On the other hand, the tips are independent and self-contained if you prefer to dip into them in a different order, as and when you feel the need. Many of the tips include suggestions for further reading if you would like to follow up on any issues in more detail.

Section B

Section B contains 12 activity types each focusing on one of the main aspects of spoken word recognition. They are suitable for awareness-raising and practice of generalisable skills, not tied to any specific language points. They may be used in a section of a lesson specifically set aside for work on pronunciation and listening. Some of them are activity types that you can use repeatedly as warmers and fillers in lessons.

Section C

Section C contains the main body of teaching materials and ideas in this book. They consist of 18 lessons exploring word recognition for listening, organised according to words which share similar features of pronunciation. Lexis provides a natural organising principle for lessons which focus on spoken word recognition. There are certain syllables which are frequently found at the start or end of words, and familiarity with these can help learners to listen more fluently. Each lesson in this section focuses on one or more of these word segments. For each lesson, there are various activities to choose from – you don't have to use them all. They can be used as stand-alone lessons, or integrated into lessons with a focus on vocabulary.

Section D

The last section of the book includes miscellaneous material which may be of interest:

- Reference chart of phonemic symbols
- Glossary of terms
- Bibliography
- Meet the Author
- Acknowledgements
- About PronPack and PronPack for Listening

Support website

Although the book is complete in itself, there is an accompanying website, www.pronpack.com, with a wealth of support materials for teachers. These include electronic reproductions of any classroom materials which appear in the book, but designed and presented in full colour so that teachers can use them in class, in printed or in digital form.

Audio material

There are audio files available for many of the activities in **sections** B and C which are indicated by the symbol ▶ . These files may be downloaded from www.pronpack.com, whether you decide to use them in class or would just like to hear them yourself in preparation for the class.

Note: Many of the audios are also available as videos on YouTube https://www.youtube.com/@PronPack

Section A Practical tips

In this section, you will find material for 12 practical tips with advice and suggestions about how to teach various aspects of spoken word recognition.

You can read this section straight through for a complete overview of the issues involved in teaching spoken word recognition. On the other hand, the tips are independent and self-contained if you prefer to dip into them in a different order, as and when you feel the need.

A1 Teach Spoken Word Recognition

In this tip, we examine the meaning of the phrase *spoken word recognition*, and look at the key concepts behind each of the three words in this phrase.

Spoken word recognition

In the field of listening, *spoken word recognition* is a technical term, sometimes abbreviated to the acronym SWP. To get the general idea of what it means, and what this book is about, it's useful to look at the three words in the term - *spoken, word* and *recognition*. Let's look at each of them in turn…

Spoken

The spoken form of English is different from the written form, and this can lead to problems in both pronunciation and listening. Imagine trying to pronounce words like *epitome* or *Worcestershire* if you've never heard them. You will probably guess and guess wrong, as I myself did for the word *epitome*.

It's not only unusual words which are difficult – if you're a teacher of English, you've probably heard students pronounce *comfortable* like *come for table*. It's not surprising if you look at the spelling. So clearly spelling can influence pronunciation, but can it also affect listening?

The answer is yes. Listening expert Anne Cutler makes the point that, 'Many words that educated adults know have been learned from reading and may indeed never have been heard'. When these words are put away in the filing cabinet of the mind, we tend to store the pronunciation too – and if we don't know it, we invent it. As Cutler puts it, 'sometimes … the stored phonological form is quite incorrect' (Cutler, 2012 p.420). In listening, we try to recognise words by matching what we hear to our stored phonological forms of words, and if these are wrong, it's difficult to make the match. You can hear a word you know and simply not recognise it.

Conclusion: don't forget to teach the spoken form of words!

Word

In a written text, the words are easily spotted – there are gaps before and after. In a spoken text, it's not so easy – it's a continuous stream of sound; the words all run together like a 'word snake' puzzle. Try spotting the words in this one:

Manyatruewordisspokeninjest

Processing a word snake like this is the written equivalent of what listeners have to do all the time. Distinguishing the words in the stream of speech is a challenge which those of us involved in teaching languages often underestimate or ignore.

Perhaps having a technical term will help to make it a thing worthy of our attention: *lexical segmentation*.

Lexical segmentation is something that listeners have to do <u>while listening</u> – we don't wait to the end and then start doing it. This means we make predictions and then correct ourselves as we go along. For example, after the first syllable of *Many a true word*, you may predict the first word to be *men*. After the second syllable, you can revise that to *many*. The process is much like the predictive text we see on our phones. As we listen, our brains are busy trying to make sense of what we hear – it's far from being the passive process we sometimes imagine!

Conclusion: help learners with the challenge of spotting words in spoken language!

Recognition

We teachers sometimes assume that if the learners know all of the vocabulary in a listening text, they will have no problem understanding its meaning, or at least, its literal meaning. This misses out one very important step in the process: recognition. Yes, our learners won't understand a text if most of the vocabulary is unknown to them, but even if they do know the words, they might not recognise them in the acoustic form that reaches their ears. That's because the sound shape of words in natural speech is rarely the same as the idealised form they may have encountered in class – the *citation form*. The citation form is the pronunciation of a word as given in the dictionary.

The sound shapes of words vary from context to context, and from speaker to speaker. Sometimes the difference is slight, but sometimes it's dramatic. A word like *secretary*, which may have four syllables in citation form, may come out sounding something like *seketary* or *seketry* or *sectary* or even the two-syllable *sectry*. It depends on the formality of the context and the accent of the speaker. This variation is not something unusual; it's the norm. If we want to help learners to recognise words when they hear them in natural speech, we need to expose them to some of this variation so that they have had experience of it – recognition is the fruit of experience.

Conclusion: prepare learners for the kind of variation they will hear in natural speech!

Cutler, A. (2012). ***Native Listening : Language Experience and the Recognition of Spoken Words*** MIT Press

A2 Break the spell of the written form

A lack of awareness of English spelling can have a surprising impact on a learner's listening skills. This relates to the way that words are stored in the memory.

How is the written form a listening problem?

It's well known that the relationship between English spelling and pronunciation is – to put it tactfully – not very logical. Some may want to put it more strongly: 'English spelling is crazy!'. Trying to pronounce words from their written form is often a recipe for disaster – and the word *recipe* is a good example of this, as experienced teachers will have noticed. So spelling can be a pronunciation problem. But how is it also a listening problem? It's because it creates a false expectation.

Take the example of *recipe*. A learner might reasonably suppose that this word is pronounced /rɪˈsaɪp/. They may store the word in their memory along with this pronunciation. In the future, they will say it this way, and they will also expect to hear it this way. As a result, when they first hear someone say /ˈresɪpiː/, they might have difficulty understanding it – they might not even recognise it at all.

Spelling pronunciation

If you invent a pronunciation of a word based on its spelling, you are making what Adam Brown calls 'spelling pronunciation' (Brown, 2019). Speakers whose first language is English sometimes intentionally create a 'spelling pronunciation' as a way of memorising how to spell a word. For instance, if you are trying to remember how to write the word /kiː/ (*quay*), a strategy might be to deliberately remember the mispronunciation /kweɪ/. For learners of English however, the problem is often in the opposite direction – they've come across the written form of the word but they don't know how to pronounce it. They may also remember the mispronunciation /kweɪ/, but for them, it's not a strategy but a mistake. The stored 'spelling pronunciation' becomes an obstacle they will need to overcome their efforts to understand spoken English.

The power of the visual

Writing about how words are stored in memory, John Field says that 'written representations in the mind are much more robust than spoken ones' (Field, 2008 p.170). This would explain the fact that learners often persist in a 'spelling pronunciation' like *lamb* with a /b/ at the end, no matter how many times you alert them to the error. For them, the memory of the written form proves stronger than the memory of the spoken form. This is why some form of phonetic spelling can be so useful in teaching. Showing your learner the word transcribed as /læm/ or simply *lam* can lead to a moment of enlightenment: 'Oh, I see now – there <u>really</u> isn't any 'b' in the pronunciation!' Seeing the phonetic version somehow makes it 'official' for them – it 'breaks the spell', as I expressed it in the title of this tip.

Spelling rules

'Silent letters' like the 'b' in lamb are notoriously tricky – the kind of feature that is used as evidence to support the claim that English spelling is 'crazy'. However, they are a relatively minor detail. What about the rest of the spelling system? The fact is, there are rules and patterns here which might not be obvious at first, but which can be very useful for learners to become aware of. There is for example the so called 'magic e' in words like *rate, kite, note* or *cute*. Far from being silent, this 'e' shows us that these words are pronounced differently from *rat, kit, not* and *cut*. Although such spelling 'rules' (or patterns) have plenty of exceptions, they are still useful.

Guessing spelling from hearing

So far, we have only been considering the influence of spelling on pronunciation (and consequently listening). But what about the other direction? Does pronunciation influence the learner's spelling? Clearly, it does. We often see examples of 'pronunciation spelling' in students' written work. While accuracy in spelling is not one of the concerns of this book, it's worth noting that it may sometimes have an impact on listening skills. Take, for example, the task of listening and note-taking. In this context, learners may often find themselves in the situation of writing down words or names which they have never seen before. If they want to make a note of the heard instruction *Change trains at Clapham*; How are they going to write *Clapham*? John Field (2008) recommends various kinds of dictation activities for practising this skill in class, perhaps focused in such a way as they draw attention to patterns in the spelling.

In conclusion, and surprising as it may seem, when teaching listening, we cannot ignore the written form.

Brown, A. (2018). **Understanding and Teaching English Spelling.** Routledge

Field, J. (2008). **Listening in the Language Classroom.** Cambridge University Press

A3 Show how words are simplified in speech

The same processes which occur across words in connected speech also occur within individual words.

Word simplification

In Tip **A2**, we saw that the written form of words often leads to problems for both pronunciation and listening. This is because words are frequently <u>not</u> pronounced in the way you would expect from the spelling. There are various reasons for this mismatch, but one which is very important is that speakers simplify words to make them easier to say. Sounds are changed, blended or even cut altogether. This is especially the case in fast informal speech, but it happens a lot in formal speech too – sometimes, the simplified form of the word is the 'official' form (as given in the dictionary).

CONSONANTS

Elision

To make words easier to say, speakers often drop consonant sounds – a process known as elision. This very often happens to /t/ and /d/ when they occur next to other consonants, as in these examples:

Christmas, handsome, sandwich, Wednesday,

Here, the elision is so common that it has become the 'official' way of saying the words, as given in the dictionary. However, speakers <u>can</u> pronounce these letters if they are being deliberately careful. In this respect they are different from 'silent letters' like the 'b' in *comb* – this 'b' wouldn't be pronounced even by a careful speaker.

For the purposes of becoming more efficient listeners, learners should realise that the kinds of elision in the examples above are very widespread indeed, and many different consonants can be cut, not only 'd' and 't'. Here are some examples:

twenty, friends, asked, clothes, fifth, hospital, perhaps

In these examples, the elisions are not 'official' – they won't be shown in the dictionary – but they are very common, and not only in fast informal speech. As a teacher, you may feel that it would be wrong to encourage learners to simplify words in this way, but that doesn't change the fact that they will no doubt <u>hear</u> them this way from time to time.

The special case of 'r'

One particular consonant which appears in the written form but which is often absent in the spoken form is the letter 'r' in cases where there is no vowel sound after it. Here are some examples:

car, early, girl, hair, near, doctor

Accents of the world can be divided into 'rhotic' (for example, American, Scottish, Irish) and 'non-rhotic' (for example English, Australian, New Zealand). In the non-rhotic accents, the 'r' in words like the examples above is not pronounced even in the 'official' dictionary form. Listeners need to be aware of this.

Assimilation

Consonants often change under the influence of a neighbouring consonant. For example, the plural ending 's' of *cats* is /s/, but the plural ending 's' of *dogs* is /z/. The plural ending changes to be more like the consonant before it. For example, if the word ends with an unvoiced consonant like /t/, then the plural ending is also unvoiced: /s/. If the word ends with a voiced consonant like /d/, then the plural ending is also voiced: /z/. This is known as assimilation.

It is also common for a consonant to change to become more similar to the consonant which follows. For example, the /n/ of *input* is often pronounced /m/ so that it is bilabial (the lips shut) like the following /p/, which is also bilabial. Assimilation like this can work in combination with elision. In the words *sandwich* and *handbag*, the /d/ is often lost by elision, and the /n/ can change to /m/ by assimilation. As a result, they can sound like *samwich* and *hambag*.

Fusion

In words where /t/, /d/ or /s/ come before /ɪ/ or /j/, the sounds may fuse together to form /ʧ/, /dʒ/ or /ʃ/. Here are some examples:

nature, lecture, duration, sugar, station, delicious, musician, ambitious

Learner listeners may be confused by fusion if they are not expecting it because the sound is so different from the spelling.

Softening

Consonants may change in certain contexts to make transitions 'softer' within a word. For example, when the letter 't' occurs between vowels, it may be pronounced more like a /d/ or /ɾ/. Here are some examples:

city, water, daughter, beautiful, photo, pretty, better, thirty

This is sometimes called the 'flapped t', and in American English, this is the 'official' form as shown in the dictionary.

VOWELS

Elision

Elision sometimes affects vowel sounds too. This typically happens to weak vowels in the middle of longer words (known as 'lost middles' in this book). This has a significant impact on the sound of a word, because when a vowel sound is lost, a whole syllable is also lost. Here are some examples:

camera, vegetable, family, evening, interesting, perhaps, Wednesday, strawberry

In some cases, there may be accent differences, with vowel elision likely in one accent but not in another. For example, speakers in England usually drop the 'e' in *strawberry* while speakers from the USA don't.

Vowel reduction

In A10, we will see that vowels in unstressed syllables very often become the weak vowel /ə/ (or sometimes /ɪ/). This can cause significant difficulty for listeners who are not expecting it. It's also a source of variation across styles and accents of speech.

Vowels which normally remain strong may be weakened in fast, informal speech. For example, the second syllable of *yellow* may become a schwa (this informal version is sometimes spelt *yeller*).

A4 Prepare learners for word variability

Words are different in different accents and different contexts. Listeners need to store multiple versions of words in their memories in order to be flexible as listeners.

Citation forms

If you look up a word in the dictionary, you will usually find that the pronunciation is given, often one version for British and one for American. This idealised pronunciation is called the 'citation form' and learners can use it as a model to aim for in their own speech. However, in the real world, people don't usually speak in citation forms. The way a word is spoken will vary from speaker to speaker, and from context to context. Speakers all have their own accents, and they will enunciate more carefully in some contexts and more hurriedly in others.

Expectation management

When it comes to listening, if your learners are expecting to hear all of the words in 'citation form', they are going to be disappointed. That's why they so often complain that, despite many years studying English, they still understand very little when they find themselves on the streets of an English-speaking country. Somehow, as teachers, we need to manage learner expectations so that they recognise multiple versions of individual words, not just the versions given in the dictionary.

Multiple versions

Take a word like *February*. The list below shows a range of versions of this word, with the citation form at the top, and the most casual version at the bottom. You can see that the number of syllables ranges from four to two (The syllables are shown separated by full stops).

/ˈfeb.ruː.ər.i/

/ˈfeb.ruː.er.i/

/ˈfeb.juː.ər.i/

/ˈfeb.jə.wer.i/

/ˈfeb.we.ri/

/ˈfeb.jʊ.ri/

/ˈfeb.jər.i/

/ˈfeb.ri/

An exemplar view

John Field suggests that listeners don't, in fact, store citation forms in their heads, but rather, multiple examples of each word – this is what he calls an 'exemplar view' (Field, 2008 p166). These examples come from a listener's experience – their listening history. Every time we hear the word, it creates a memory trace of that particular version. Once we have that version stored, we will be much faster at recognising it when we hear something similar in the future. This is why it's much easier to understand speech in an accent that we are familiar with.

More voices in the classroom

If we accept the 'exemplar view' outlined above, there are important implications for teaching listening. We must accept variation as the norm, and make sure our learners are ready for it. As Field puts it, 'A listener who has recognised the sound [əʊ] or the word *actually* in twenty voices and twenty contexts has a stronger impression of the ways in which they vary than one who has only practised recognising them when modelled by a teacher' (Field, 2008 p.329). It seems that as far as listening is concerned, we need to bring more voices into the classroom!

Accelerated exposure

How do people become be expert listeners in their own first languages? The answer is: by many years of intensive experience and exposure to the many variations in the way words are pronounced. This is something we can't hope to replicate in the language classroom, but what we can do is try to accelerate the exposure that we make available to our learners. I'm not talking here simply about extensive listening practice, useful though this may be. I'm talking about focused exposure to repeated instances of the same words and phrases in multiple voices and contexts.

Audio concordances

In our book *Authentic Listening Resource Pack* (Hancock, M. & McDonald, A. 2014), Annie and I tried to create accelerated exposure to language chunks in multiple voices and contexts by searching through our audio material for instances of a target word or phrase, and then editing the audio. For example, we searched our collection for the phrase *a little bit*, and then copied the audio of that phrase plus a bit of co-text (a few words before and after it), and made a new audio file of all these copied fragments. The learner, on listening to this file, would gain exposure to a range of possible versions of the phrase which would take weeks to accumulate otherwise. We have called this kind of file an *audio concordance*.

YouGlish

If you have access to a collection of audio files, you can of course make your own audio concordances. The free online audio-editing tool *Audacity* can be used for this purpose. However, there's no doubt that it is labour-intensive. There's a much easier alternative which you can use in class, or point your learners to for homework, and this is the online tool *YouGlish*. This is essentially a searchable corpus of online video material. You simply type in a word like *February* or a phrase like *a little bit*, and the app will play thousands of segments of video featuring that fragment, in multiple voices and contexts. This is exactly what learners need to gain accelerated exposure to the various ways these bits of language may sound in context. Just what the doctor ordered!

Field, J. (2008). **Listening in the Language Classroom.** Cambridge University Press

Hancock, M. & McDonald, A. (2014) **Authentic Listening Resource Pack.** Delta Publishing

A5 Highlight the structure of syllables

Learner-listeners need to become familiar with the typical structure of syllables in English. These may differ from the syllable forms they are familiar with in their first language.

What are syllables?

To keep things simple in this tip, we will just look at words which consist of just one syllable, leaving consideration of longer words for **A6**. Say this one-syllable word repeatedly:

knock knock knock knock knock knock!

Notice that the word sounds like the thing it refers to – it is onomatopoeic. It is a series of loud sounds (like a knuckle hitting a door) separated by quieter sounds or silences. The loud sounds correspond to the letter 'o' in the word – the vowel. This is a good way of thinking of a syllable: the loudest part is the vowel in the middle. The consonants on either side of it (if there are any) are relatively quiet.

The parts of a syllable

A syllable consists of three parts – these are: **1.** onset; **2.** peak; **3.** coda

The essential part is the peak in the middle – the vowel sound. Some syllables only a peak by itself, for example *eye*. The onset is one or more consonant sounds before the vowel (for example /fr/ in *free*) and the coda is one or more consonant sounds after it (for example /gz/ in *eggs*).

There are rules about which consonant sounds may appear in the onset and coda, and these vary from language to language. For example, in English, the 'ng' sound /ŋ/ can not occur in the onset and the /h/ cannot occur in the coda. The rules may vary across accents too: the /r/ does not appear in the coda in most accents of England, Australia and New Zealand, but it does in most accents of North America, Scotland and Ireland.

Short vowel sounds need a coda

If the peak of a syllable is one of the short (or 'lax') vowels - /æ, e, ɪ, ʌ, ʊ/ (plus /ɒ/ for British English) – there <u>must</u> be a consonant sound after it in English. English words never end in a short vowel sound. They <u>can</u> end in a single vowel letter, but it will be pronounced as a long vowel or diphthong, for example, *hi* /haɪ/, *me* /miː/, *spa* /spɑː/, *do* /duː/. We also often find weak vowels sounds like /ə/ (schwa) at the end of one-syllable function words such as *the*.

Listeners can and do use this kind of knowledge to help identify word boundaries. For example, if you hear the sound sequence /getʌp/, you know there could be a word boundary after the /t/ (get up). However, there can't be one before the /t/ because /ge/ is not a possible word in English (because it ends with the short vowel sound /e/).

Spelling versus pronunciation

If you are telling learners about syllable structure in English, make sure you distinguish clearly between spelling and pronunciation, otherwise things can get very confused. For example, the syllable *white* ends with a vowel letter but a consonant sound. Notice that the letters 'y' and 'w' represent consonant sounds when they are in the onset of a syllable, as in *yes* and *wear*, but they represent vowel sounds when they are in the peak, as in *try* or *known*.

Consonant clusters

Different languages have different 'rules' about what combinations of consonants can occur in the onset and coda of syllables. For example, English syllables don't like to start with combinations like *mp*, *nd*, *nk*, *lt*, *ts*, or *ps*. They don't like to end with combinations like *sl*, *str*, *sn*, *tr*, *cl* or *tw*.

Awareness of such 'rules' can help listeners decide where the boundaries between words lie. For example, if you hear the cluster /ps/, you know it can't be the start of a new word. If you hear the cluster /tr/, you know it can't be the end of a word. Other languages, such as Polish, may be perfectly happy to accept such combinations.

Syllable structure in different languages

The rules of syllable structure are often different in different languages, and this can have an effect on the way learners from other language backgrounds hear and pronounce English. For example, in languages such as Spanish and Portuguese, the consonant cluster /sk/ cannot occur in the onset of a syllable. When learners from these language backgrounds hear an English word like *school*, instead of hearing it as one syllable /skuːl/, they hear it as two syllables: /es.kuːl/. Now, the /s/ is the coda of the first syllable and /k/ is the onset of the second. Because they perceive it this way, they pronounce it this way, as anybody who has taught Spanish and Portuguese-speaking learners will know. At some point in their learning journey, such learners will need to begin to accept that English syllables can begin with consonant clusters like /sk/.

A6 Know how to divide words into syllables

There are different possible ways of dividing words into syllables. Decide which method you prefer and try to be consistent.

The importance of syllables

In spoken word recognition, it seems that syllables are a very salient feature for listeners – they are like the building blocks of words. People usually have an intuitive sense of how many syllables a word contains, and that's enough for most purposes. However, if you are teaching pronunciation, it's often useful to be able to separate the syllables of a word. Since there is more than one way to do this, it's best to choose one and be consistent. In Tip **A5**, we looked at what the defining features of individual syllables in the context of one-syllable words. Here we will look at how to divide up words of more than one syllable.

Showing syllable divisions

Dictionaries and teaching materials often show syllable boundaries with full stops – for example /ˈen.teʳ.teɪn.mənt/. This gives learners a very helpful visual impression of how the word sounds. But how do the authors know where to put these divisions? And how do we know where to put the divisions for ourselves, when writing on the board for example? Sometimes it's intuitively easy, but sometimes not, and not everybody does it in the same way.

Two principles

In dividing words into syllables, people commonly use one or both of the following principles:

1. **If in doubt, consonants go right:** Make each syllable begin with a consonant sound if possible. If there is just one consonant sound between two vowel sounds, attach it to the syllable on the right. For example, in the word *about*, attach the consonant /b/ to the second syllable: *a.bout* (not *ab.out*).

2. **Every syllable should be possible as single word:** Don't create syllables which would be impossible as a single word. For example, don't split *singing* into *si.nging* /sɪ.ŋɪŋ/. As we saw in **A5**, a content word can't end with a short vowel like /ɪ/, and no word can begin with /ŋ/ in English. Instead, split this word like this: *sing.ing* /sɪŋ.ɪŋ/.

Principles in conflict

Sometimes the two principles of syllable division are in conflict. For example, by **Principle 1**, we would divide *money* as *mo.ney*. However, this is not allowed by **Principle 2**, because /mʌ/ ends with a short vowel and so it's not a possible word. In this book, we will say that in cases of conflict, we go with **Principle 2**, so *money* would be *mon.ey*. This follows the convention often used in reference materials such as *The Cambridge English Pronouncing Dictionary*. However, as a teacher, you may have a strong preference for **Principle 1** in <u>all</u> cases – if so, you will need to adapt some of the games and activities in this book to reflect that.

Syllable activities

The reason that you may want to divide words into syllables is to break down long words into shorter building blocks, so that learners can pronounce them *bit-by-bit*. You may also find yourself wanting to write words broken down into syllables in boardwork, or in making your own teaching materials. For example, you could have matching activities where the learners have to match syllables together to make words from jumbled lists like this:

1st syllable: *cin*, *hol*, *sal*

2nd syllable: a, e, i

3rd syllable: ry, ma, day

*Answers: **cin**ema, **hol**iday, **sal**ary*

You will find more examples of syllable activities in **Sections B** and **C**, where they are there for the purpose of raising learner awareness of typical syllable shapes in English. This, according to John Field, makes an important contribution toward learners' listening fluency.

Syllables without vowels?

As we saw in **A5**, a vowel sound is the only essential part of a syllable. However, that's not entirely true. We occasionally find syllables with <u>no</u> vowel in the peak. Take for example the second syllable in *couldn't*. While some speakers put the weak vowel sound /ə/ between the 'd' and the 'n', many other speakers don't insert any vowel at all. In this case, the 'n' becomes the peak of the syllable (this is known as a *syllabic consonant*). However, this is a detail you don't necessarily need to complicate your class with, unless the learners have a special interest in that kind of thing.

Field, J. (2008). ***Listening in the Language Classroom***. Cambridge University Press

Jones, Roach, Setter & Esling , (2011). ***The Cambridge English Pronouncing Dictionary*** Cambridge University Press

A7 Pay attention to word stress

Word stress helps listeners to identify words. The stressed syllable is noticeable either by being longer, louder or higher, or by having a strong vowel rather than a weak one.

Stress patterns

In any word of two or more syllables, one of the syllables will be 'stressed' – it is made more noticeable by being longer, louder and different in pitch than the others. For example, *banana* has three syllables and the second is stressed. The stress pattern of this word could be represented by big and small circles like this: **oOo**. The stress pattern is part of what makes the word recognisable, along with the sequence of phonemes. It is usually indicated in the dictionary with an apostrophe before the stressed syllable, for example /bəˈnɑːnə/ or /bəˈnænə/.

Strong vowel sounds

We saw above that stress is created by making one of the syllables longer, louder or different in pitch from the others. However, in a longer phrase, this may get lost. For example, in *a banana milk shake*, we may not hear the word stress *banana*. However, the second syllable remains noticeable because the of the vowel sound: it's stronger than the vowel sounds in the other syllables of the word. We should bear in mind then that word stress is often mostly identifiable because of the quality of the vowel sound rather than on account of the stress *per se*. What this means in practical terms is that when teaching word stress in class, we should pay attention not only to the stress, but also how stress affects the vowel sounds in words.

Word stress and listening

From a listener's perspective, a stressed syllable (with its strong vowel) can be an 'island of reliability' in the stream of speech. Unstressed syllables tend to be weak and less easy to make out while stressed syllables maintain their characteristic sound. Because of this, stressed syllables are often the listener's key to recognising words in English, and learners need to become aware of this.

Stress deafness

In English, word stress can be used by listeners to help them identify words, and so their ears are primed to notice this feature. This does not happen in all languages. In languages where word stress is not a feature, or where it always occurs on the same syllable – the last one, for example, listeners may not pay much attention to it. Learners from these L1 backgrounds may be *stress deaf* in English – that is, unable to perceive it, to begin with at least. This puts them at a disadvantage as listeners in English.

Stress minimal pairs

A good way to oblige learners to pay attention to word stress is to use activities where pairs of words are distinguished by the stress.

For example, in the activity in *Figure 1*, the sentences in columns **A** and **B** are distinguishable only by the stress in the final word – they are effectively minimal pairs, with verbs in **A** and the corresponding nouns in **B**. In this activity, you read out one of the sentences randomly and learners listen and identify if it's from **A** or **B**. This activity is from *PronPack 3: Pronunciation Pairworks*. Notice that in the phonemic transcription, we can see the vowel changes which are caused by changing the stress in the words.

Figure 1.

A oO	B Oo
1. The workers protest /prə'test/	The worker's protest /'prəʊtest/
2. The families rebel /rɪ'bəl/	The family's rebel /'rebəl/
3. Their stories conflict /kən'flɪkt/	Their story's conflict /'kɒnflɪkt/
4. The countries export /ɪk'spɔː(r)t/	The country's export /'ekspɔː(r)t/

Stressed syllable dictation

John Field suggests a form of dictation where you say only the stressed syllable of words and the learners have to listen and complete the word. Here are some of the examples he gives (Field 2008):

> *morn* (morning), *twen* (twenty), *dif* (different/difficult), *ques* (question), *pose* (suppose)

There may sometimes be more than one possibility, of course, but the activity is intended to demonstrate that hearing the stressed syllable is often enough to identify or predict the whole word. You can make it easier by telling the student if the syllable is at the start, middle or end of the word. You could also limit the words to certain categories, for example months and dates, or words relating to a discipline such as economics.

Field, J. (2008). ***Listening in the Language Classroom.*** Cambridge University Press

Hancock, M. (2017) ***PronPack 3: Pronunciation Pairworks.*** Hancock McDonald ELT

A8 Highlight stress patterns and variation

Word stress in English does not obey simple rules, but there are some useful patterns to learn. We also need to bear in mind some of the ways that stress patterns vary across accents and contexts.

Stress patterns

As soon as a word has more than one syllable, it will have a stress pattern which is created by its combination of stressed and unstressed syllables. For example, *sofa* has the pattern **Oo** while *relax* has the pattern **oO**. These patterns are part of the character of the word – something that will help the listener to recognise it in the flow of speech.

Stress and word class

Learners are often disappointed to learn that there aren't any easy rules which tell you where to put the stress in English words – you basically have to learn the stress patterns for each word, one by one. However, there <u>are</u> patterns which are useful to know, providing we remember that there are plenty of exceptions. One important pattern relates to word class:

– **Nouns** don't like having stress at the end:

donkey, **ti**ger, **dol**phin, **oc**topus, **black**bird, go**ri**lla
(but note exceptions eg. gi**raffe**, chimpan**zee**)

– **Verbs** are quite happy to have stress at the end:

a**llow**, collect, migrate, arrive, increase, protect, relax
(but note exceptions eg. *offer, visit, answer*)

Stress and suffixes

One area where we can make useful generalisations about word stress relates to morphology, and in particular, suffixes. While some suffixes can be added and do not alter the stress in the root word (*stress-neutral*), others cause the stress in the root word to change in a predictable way (*stress-shifting*). Here are some examples of each:

stress-neutral: *-ful, -ness, -able, -less, -ment, -ise, -al, -ish, -ship*

stress-shifting: *-ity, -tion, -ic, -ology, -graphy*

Stress in word families

As a result of adding suffixes of the two kinds above, we find 'families' of related words which do not have the stress on the same syllable. Here are some examples:

democrat – de**mo**cracy – demo**cra**tic

photograph – pho**tog**raphy – photo**graph**ic

celebrate – ce**leb**rity – cele**bra**tion

Listeners need to be aware of the differences in stress in word families like this, and perhaps most importantly, the resulting differences in the vowel sounds. For example, the first vowel in democrat is a full vowel (/e/) while the second is the weak vowel /ə/. In democracy, this is reversed – the first is a weak vowel (/ə/ or /ɪ/) and the second is a full vowel (/ɒ/ or /ɑ/).

Symmetry

In words of two syllables, one of the syllables is unstressed, and the vowel in this syllable is often reduced to a schwa – for example, tiger /ˈtaɪgəʳ/ and collect /kəˈlekt/. In these cases, the stress pattern is very asymmetrical: the weak syllable is <u>much</u> weaker than the strong one.

However, in many words, the vowel sound in the unstressed syllable is not reduced, for example, blackbird /ˈblækbɜːd/ and migrate /maɪˈgreɪt/. In these cases, the stress pattern is more symmetrical – the unstressed syllable is still quite strong.

In English, listeners are more sensitive to stress errors in the asymmetrical words. Errors in symmetrical words don't seem to affect intelligibility much.

Accent variation

Words with more symmetry in the stress pattern sometimes differ from accent to accent. For example, migrate has the pattern **oO** for most British speakers **Oo** for most American speakers. It seems like for the American speaker, there's a magnet pulling the stressed syllable to the left, towards the start of the word. The same effect can be seen in words like cigarette, magazine and chimpanzee, which have the stress at the end for British speakers and the beginning for Americans. The opposite happens in words which are imported directly from French such as cliché or ballet – here, American speakers leave the stress at the end (as in French), while British speakers pull it to the beginning. Listeners need to be flexible enough to deal with stress variation in words like this.

Stress shift

Sometimes the stress pattern of a word may change when it is in context. For example, the stress pattern for fourteen is **oO**, but in the context of a phrase like fourteen people it may change to **Oo**. The reason for this relates to rhythm: English prefers to alternate stressed and unstressed syllables where possible – the pattern **OoOo** is preferable to **oOOo**. As a result, the stress in fourteen shifts to the first syllable in fourteen people – this is known as stress shift. Because fourteen has a fairly symmetrical stress pattern, this shift doesn't seem to affect the intelligibility of the word.

A9 Raise awareness of weak syllables

Syllables with weak vowels are hard to hear and can make words sound very different from what learners expect. Learners need to be aware of them and familiar with how they sound in words.

Schwa

There is one vowel sound which is greatly responsible for the characteristic sound of English – the weak vowel sound /ə/ (often called *schwa*). This sound behaves in a different way from strong vowel sounds. Strong vowels play a role in distinguishing one word from another – for example, *man* and *men* are distinguished only by the vowel sounds. The schwa, on the other hand, plays no such distinguishing role. Instead, it can substitute for any of the other vowel sounds when they occur in an unstressed syllable. For example, the second syllable in hurricane is unstressed. For some speakers, this syllable has a strong vowel: /ˈhʌrɪkeɪn/. For other speakers, it is replaced by schwa: / ˈhʌrɪk(ə)n/. The *Cambridge Pronouncing Dictionary* gives both possibilities.

The familiarity effect

In the example of *hurricane*, we saw that speakers could choose between a full vowel and a reduced form. One of the reasons they might choose to do the latter could be called *the familiarity effect*. Pronunciation of words and names often vary among speakers depending on familiarity. This is very noticeable with place names. For example, the second syllable of the Australian cities *Brisbane* and *Melbourne* will be identical for many speakers, with a weak vowel sound: /bən/. However, speakers who are less familiar with these places may pronounce them using a 'spelling pronunciation' (pronouncing them as they appear in written form, with full vowels).

A priority for listening

In the example of *hurricane*, we saw that in the unstressed syllable the dictionary gave schwa as an alternative to a strong vowel: the schwa is optional. However, in many cases schwa is given as the only possibility with no alternative. For example, *Canada* is given as /ˈkanədə/, with schwa as the second and third vowel sound. Does this mean then that */ˈkænædæ/ would be unintelligible? Actually, it doesn't; it would almost certainly be intelligible to a listener. Indeed, speakers may pronounce it this way in order to be heard more clearly – in a noisy environment for example (this is known as *hyper-articulation*).

If your learner's goal is simply to be understood, you don't need to insist that they use schwa in all the same places that native speakers of the UK and US would use them.

Indeed, in some varieties of English, such as West African English, vowel reduction is much less frequent. However, the schwa is very common – it is said to be the most common vowel sound in English. For this reason, learners will surely need to be able to deal with it in their listening.

The other reduced vowel

The /ə/ (*schwa*) is the only vowel sound which is <u>exclusively</u> found in unstressed syllables – that is its defining feature. However, there's another vowel sound which is sometimes strong but sometimes weak like schwa, namely /ɪ/. In the word *chicken* /ˈtʃɪkɪn/, /ɪ/ is strong in the first syllable but weak in the second. Where it's a weak sound, some speakers use a schwa instead: /ˈtʃɪkən/ – the two weak vowels are often interchangeable that way.

Disappearing schwa

The weak vowels can be a challenge to listeners because they may be so weak as to be almost imperceptible. Indeed, the schwa may be reduced so much that it effectively disappears, thus removing a syllable from a word. This sometimes happens to unstressed middle syllables – for example, words like *family* and *history* may sound like *famly* and *histry*. In this book, we call this phenomenon 'lost middles' – see **A3** and **B11**.

Easier for the speaker, harder for the listener

From a speaker's perspective, weak vowels make life easier because these vowels don't require a lot of muscular effort to articulate. From a learner-listener's perspective, however, the story is different. Weak vowels are indistinct and often mean that words sound different from what learners <u>expect</u> to hear. Moreover, vowel reduction can create ambiguity. For example, when the unstressed vowel is reduced to /ə/, the words *saver* and *savour* sound identical – they become *homophones*. Vowel reduction in English is a major difficulty in spoken word recognition for learners of the language.

Conclusions

In order to improve as a listener in English, a learner will need to learn to cope with weak vowels. Teachers can do things to help with this:

1 raise awareness of weak vowels,

2 manage expectations, so that learners don't expect to hear full vowels in all syllables of a word,

3 encourage learners to be tolerant of ambiguity in homophones and near-homophones, and to use context to help them decide the meaning in these cases.

Jones, Roach, Setter & Esling, (2011). *The Cambridge English Pronouncing Dictionary* Cambridge University Press

A10 Raise the awareness of rhythm

In the rhythm of English, there are often a large number of weak syllables squeezed between two stressed syllables. Because these segments are particularly hard to hear, they can cause learner-listeners to panic.

Syllables, stress and rhythm

The rhythm of English is created by the pattern of syllables and stress. Compared to many other languages, the stressed syllables are more emphatic while the weak syllables are more reduced. This means that there's a bigger contrast between the strong and weak syllables. This contrast creates rhythms which can be represented by big and small circles:

OO – *Sleep well*
OoO – *Mind the gap*
OooO – *Give me a ring*

In the examples above, each circle happens to represent a separate word, but individual words and phrases also have similar rhythmic patterns:

oO – *coffee shop*
OooO – *cinema lights*
OoooOo – *supermarket trolley*

Stumbling blocks

Weak syllables are sometimes put under pressure. When there are two or more of them sandwiched between two stressed syllables they may be forced into a shorter period of time. For example, the time allowed for the three weak syllables in **OoooO** may be not much more than the time allowed for the single weak syllable in **OoO**. In this context, syllables are often mutilated – consonants change or get cut, and vowels are often reduced or lost. Richard Cauldwell calls these areas of multiple weak syllables 'squeeze zones' (Cauldwell, 2018), and they are very challenging for learner-listeners.

Listener's panic

People who are learning a foreign language often feel a sense of panic when confronted with listening to non-simplified speech. The speech is perceived as being sadistically fast, and learners often feel a lack of control – you can't usually pause the speech or slow it down or listen again. This may be true for all languages, but it's also probably true that each language has its own special way of being 'difficult'. I think that for English, this special difficulty lies in the rhythm of the language, and in particular, the 'squeeze zones'. Learners perceive that a lot of syllables have gone by quickly which they have not been able to 'catch'. They suppose that they are therefore missing important information and despair sets in.

What do the experts do?

You may wonder, if these squeeze zones are so difficult, how expert listeners manage to make any sense of them. The answer is that expert listeners are <u>used to</u> squeeze zones, and that's because they are <u>predictable</u>. When you know what's going to be said, you don't need to clearly hear all the detail.

Let's take a simple example: the word *predictable*. We could represent the stress pattern of this word as **oOoo**. As you can see, the word ends with two consecutive weak syllables, and depending what word comes next, this could become a squeeze zone. Those two weak syllables may be hard to hear, but it won't matter: the expert listener hears the root word *predict*, and knows that like many verbs, this may be turned into an adjective by the addition of the suffix *able*. Having heard this suffix many times before, our listener doesn't need to hear the syllables clearly – just a couple of indistinct pulses will do. The speaker knows this, and so doesn't have to make an effort to enunciate the syllables clearly, and a squeeze zone is born.

What teachers can do?

If the secret of the expert listener's skill is basically long experience, then perhaps there's little we can do in the classroom to help our learners. If it's all about experience, then it's just a question of listen, listen, and more listen. However, I think it may be possible to <u>accelerate</u> experience by exploiting the predictability of squeeze zones.

Accelerated experience

In the example of *predictable*, we saw that the suffix *able* is something that listeners can anticipate, and something they will have heard a lot of times before. They are familiar with the rhythm of it – that characteristic pair of pulses at the end of a root word. What if we try to help our learners become familiar with that rhythm too? We could do this by using a text which includes an unusually high density of that very feature. Here's an example – a short text in the form of a rhyme:

> They're **comfo**rtable and **dur**able
> They're **lov**able, **ad**orable
> **Fashio**nable but **sens**ible
> To **me** they're indis**pens**able

Earworms

Because the sound sequence /əbəl/ (or /əbl̩/) is repeated so many times in the short text above, learners can't help but notice its characteristic sound and rhythm. You can say it, or play a recording, while learners listen. You can also get learners to try reciting the text themselves. I call these short texts with a concentration of a given feature 'earworms', and there are plenty to be found in **Section C** of this book.

Cauldwell, R. (2018). *A Syllabus for Listening – Decoding* Speech in Action

A11 Help learners to spot word boundaries

Unlike in writing, there are not usually gaps before and after words in spoken English. Learners can benefit from using strategies to spot words in the flow of speech.

What do the experts do?

Spoken language is usually a continuous stream of sound, without gaps between words. Expert listeners have strategies to help them identify the beginnings and ends of words. These 'lexical segmentation' strategies vary from language to language. Here we will focus on strategies used in English to:

1 identify word beginnings.

2 identify word endings.

1 Identifying word beginnings

To illustrate a point about the importance of word stress, Anne Cutler gives us this infuriating little limerick (Cutler, 2012 p.130):

> A **lim**erick's **rhy**thm is **best**
> With the **strong**est of **syll**ables **stressed**
> If you **let** the stress **fall**
> On a **weak** syllable
> All your **read**ers will **right**ly pro**test**

Readers will 'rightly protest' that this poem forces you to stress the final syllable of *syllable*, which is wrong. It's so wrong that if you were listening rather than reading the limerick, you might not even recognise the word. You might think that line 4 is talking about a *weak silly ball*, for example.

Stressed first syllables

Word stress generally helps listeners to recognise words, as the limerick illustrates. But also, and more specifically, it helps us to recognise where a new word begins.

Statistically, there is over 90% chance that if you hear a stressed syllable in English, it's the beginning of a word, and this is a fact that expert listeners use to help them in lexical segmentation (Cutler, 2012). In the limerick, we can see that, correctly pronounced, all but the last word in the poem indeed have the stress on the first syllable.

Expert listeners pay attention to word stress, and if we can get learners to do the same (as suggested in **A7**), we will also be helping them to make use of an important clue in word-boundary recognition.

Unstressed first syllables
If you decide to share the 90% statistic above with learners, you could also show them that there is often a pattern to the exceptions too:

A We saw in **A7** that there is a strong tendency for verbs in English not to have the stress at the beginning, as illustrated by the word *protest* in the limerick. In fact, there are a limited number of these verbal first syllables which occur over and over again, so it's worth drawing learner attention to them. To this end, you could use the material in **B4** of this book, as well as **C6**, **C7** and **C8**.

B There are some common prefixes in English which are unstressed. These are word beginnings which can be added to root word to change its meaning – most notably *un-* (*unhappy*) and *in-* (*incorrect*) or *im-* (*impossible*).

2 Identifying word endings
Here's a limerick which hopefully will not cause readers to protest, because the word stress falls where it's supposed to. This one is from **C14** in this book:

*This **fam**ous young **cook** from Maurit**ious***
*Was **anx**ious but **al**so amb**it**ious*
*His **house** is not grac**ious***
*His **kitch**en's not **spac**ious*
*But **man**, are his **dish**es del**ic**ious!*

You'll notice that the poem contains many words with the same syllable at the end, namely /əs/. For some of these words, the word ending is a recognisable suffix – something which can be added to a root word, like *ous* being added to *fame*. For others, the ending is not obviously a suffix – for example, it's not obvious what the root word is for *ambitious*. However, the important point is this: there are certain typical word endings in English which a lot of words share. Most of these endings will be unstressed syllables, often with reduced vowels, so they can be difficult to hear clearly. However, if we can help learners to notice how these endings sound, we will be providing them with a clue for identifying where words end. This is an important element in the skill of word boundary recognition, or 'lexical segmentation', and it's the main objective of the majority of the lessons in **Section C** of this book.

Cutler, A. (2012). Native Listening : ***Language Experience and the Recognition of Spoken Words.*** MIT Press

A12 Encourage active listening

Expert listeners actively interpret the meaning of a message at the same time as they are hearing it.

Active listening

Most of us are familiar with the experience of hearing songs wrongly. Situations like this: you've always thought that the singer Madonna was saying 'Poppadom peach', only to discover to your surprise that in fact she was saying 'Papa, don't preach'. On reflection, you may wonder how you could ever have accepted the 'poppadom peach' interpretation – it seems so surreal! Perhaps it's because you were hearing the lyric but not really paying attention; when we listen actively, we work harder to make sense of things.

Multi-tasking

Here's a simplified model of what listening involves:

1 The listener receives a sound sequence through the ear ('decoding')

2 The listener converts the sound sequence into meaning ('meaning-building')

The simplicity of the model is appealing, but also misleading. It gives the impression that **Step 1** is complete before **Step 2** begins. In fact, both steps are happening at the same time. The listener is developing an idea of what the message is about even before it's actually finished – and indeed they must do this. On top of that, the mind of the listener needs to be actively predicting what will come next at the same time – it's a kind of multi-tasking.

Provisional interpretation

An important implication of the mental multi-tasking described above is that the listener will often predict wrongly and then have to revise their understanding. The interpretation has to be provisional. Here's an example:

a. /ɪtsəˈfɪʃ.../ = It's a fish…
b. /ɪtsəˈfɪʃəl/ = It's official!

Let's say you hear the unfinished sound sequence in **a.** above. You may decide that the speaker is saying It's a fish. Then, a moment later, the message is completed as in **b.** This will mean returning to what you've just heard (which is stored in your 'working memory') and revising your interpretation to It's official.

Working memory

There is more than one kind of memory. There is long-term memory, which has a huge capacity. But according to Field, there is also 'working memory', which we use for processing language while listening. This kind of memory is short-term and has a more limited capacity. Expert listeners make predictions, but they keep an open mind and revise their predictions where necessary. This constant revision makes heavy demands on the working memory. Learner listeners, on the other hand, tend to have less working memory to spare, with so much of their attention taken up in making sense of the unfamiliar language. This means that they are often less flexible, clinging to their first interpretation in a panicky reflex. Result: our expert listener goes with *official*; our learner sticks with *fish*, even if it's surreal in the context. They need to get into the habit of revising their understanding more readily.

Active listening work in the classroom

If learners wish to become more expert in their listening, they will need to become active listeners. They will need to develop their ability to multi-task in the ways outlined above. This is challenging, given the limitations of working memory. However, at least we can begin by making learners aware of some of the steps involved in reaching that goal. Let's look at two classroom activities which we can use with this in mind:

1 Predicting how the speaker will continue.

2 Revising earlier predictions in the light of what comes after.

1 Predicting how the speaker will continue

If you are using an audio in class for listening practice, pause the audio at random moments and ask the learners to suggest what the speaker will say next. Accept any of the following suggestions:

- complete a word which was cut off by the pause
- say what the next word or words will be
- complete a phrase which was cut off by the pause
- say in your own words what the speaker will talk about next

It's highly likely that some of the predictions that you get from the class will be accurate. Take the opportunity to point out that good listeners are constantly guessing at what will come next while they listen.

2 Revising earlier predictions in the light of what comes after

This activity can be an extension of the previous one. After pausing an audio and hearing the learners' predictions of what will come next, make no comment; simply play the next few moments of the audio and ask them to say if it confirms any of the predictions or not.

An alternative procedure is to do a dictation activity based on sentence stems and complete sentences, like the example mentioned above:

a. /ɪtsəˈfɪʃ.../ = *It's a fish...*
b. /ɪtsəˈfɪʃəl/ = *It's official!*

First, say the sentence stem **a**, and ask learners to write what they hear. Then explain that you are going to say the same phrase again plus the ending. Ask them to either:

– complete what they wrote in the first part of the dictation.

– correct what they wrote and complete it.

There are plenty more examples of these stem-plus-completion dictations in this book, in an activity-type labelled 'trictation'.

Field, J. (2008). ***Listening in the Language Classroom.*** Cambridge University Press

Section B Word recognition games

In this section, you will find material for 12 lessons, each focusing on a key aspect of spoken word recognition.

These lessons are suitable for raising awareness of aspects of spoken word recognition. They may be used in a section of a lesson specifically set aside for work on pronunciation and listening. Some of them are activity types that you can use repeatedly as warmers and fillers in lessons.

Audio files
There are audio files available for any activities which are indicated by the symbol ▶. These can be downloaded from the **Resources** section for this book on the PronPack website.

Worksheets
For any of the activities which require handouts or slides to share with your learners, these are available and downloadable from the **Resources** section for this book on the PronPack website.

B1 Open syllable maze

This activity aims to raise awareness of possible syllable shapes in English, and the correspondence of sound and spelling.

Background: content words of one syllable

1 All content words of one syllable have a vowel sound at the centre – some are only a vowel: *eye, owe*

2 Syllables may have one or more consonant before the vowel, for example: *go, me, toe, fly, high*

3 Syllables which don't have any consonant after the vowel such as the examples in 2, are known as 'open syllables'.

4 Syllables may also have consonant sounds at the end, and these are called 'closed syllables': *got, met, toast, flight, laugh*

5 If the vowel in the syllable is a short vowel (/æ, e, ɪ, ʌ, ʊ/ and also /ɒ/ for British English), then there <u>must</u> be a consonant after it – it must be 'closed', for example: *cat, bet, lip, cup* and for British English, *lost*

The game

In this game, learners have to find a path though a maze. All of the words in the maze are content words of just one syllable. Some of them are 'open syllables' (ending with a vowel sound) and some of them are 'closed syllables' (ending with a consonant sound). In this maze, you can only step on stones which contain open syllables. The challenge is to recognise which words end with a vowel sound – it's not always obvious from the spelling!

> **Answers:** *go – me – spa – flu – ski – (car) – do – blue – sea – too – shoe – toe – fly – draw – buy – high – how – see.*

Follow up

When the learners have finished the maze and you have checked the answers together, you can point out one or more of the following observations to them:

1 The first words in the correct path (*go, me, spa, flu, ski, do*) all contain a single vowel letter. Single vowel letters usually spell a short vowel in the middle of a word, but at the end of a word they are long vowels. (One-syllable content words never end with a short vowel) Note: The word 'car' is open in accents where the 'r' is not pronounced, and closed in accents where the 'r' is pronounced, so it's optional in this game.

2 The next words in the correct path (*blue, sea, too, shoe, toe, see*) all end with pairs of vowel letters. These normally spell long vowels (including diphthongs).

3 The next words in the correct path (*fly, draw, buy, how*) end with the letters 'y' or 'w'. At the end of a word, these letters represent vowel sounds, so these are open syllables.

4 The word *high* ends with a vowel sound including silent 'gh' spelling. Be careful – this is not always silent – for example, in laugh and cough, it represents /f/.

5 Many of the closed syllables in this maze end with the vowel letter 'e'. This is known as the 'magic e' – it's not pronounced at the end of the word, but it may change the vowel sound in the middle of the word. For example, compare the pronunciations of the words *site* and *sit*.

Optional final challenge: find words in the game beginning or ending with <u>more</u> than one consonant sounds! (**Answers:** *fly, draw, spa, style, flu, blue, ski, smile, six*).

B1 Open Syllable Maze

Go from **GO** to **SEE**. You can only step on words which end with a vowel sound (these are called 'open syllables')

(Be careful: think about pronunciation, not spelling. Some words finish with a consonant letter but a vowel sound (eg. fly). Some words finish with a vowel letter but a consonant sound (eg. site)

Answers: *go – me – spa – flu – ski – (car) – do – blue – sea – too – shoe – toe – fly – draw – buy – high – how – see.*

B2 Cluster maps

This activity aims to focus attention on syllables including consonant clusters which are possible in English but perhaps not in the learners' L1.

Background

At the heart of a syllable is a vowel sound. For example, the word *owe* is a syllable which is nothing more than a vowel sound. Added to this there may be consonant sounds at the beginning (for example, *low*, *flow*, *snow*) and at the end (for example, *owes*, *old*, *hoped*). Where there is more than one consonant together, it's known as a consonant cluster. Experienced listeners know which consonant clusters are 'allowed' at the beginning or end of a syllable and use that to help recognise words. For example, in English, if you hear /str/ you know it's the start of a syllable, not the end. If you hear /ps/, you know it's the end of a syllable, not the start.

The Game

In this game, learners have to look at a street map, and follow instructions to find one of the places a – i on the map. The difficulty is that the names of the streets are similar-sounding. In order to succeed, the listener must be able to distinguish between consonant clusters. In the first version of the game (Map 1) the clusters are at the start of the words, and in the second version (Map 2), the clusters are at the end.

1 Give or show learners the map. Point out the streets one by one and read out the name to familiarise them with the pronunciation. They will notice that the three horizontal streets sound quite similar and the three vertical streets too.

2 Write an example sentence on the board. For Map 1, this could be:
   Let's meet at the corner of State Street and Stream Street.
   Ask learners to identify which place on the map this refers to (Answer = b).

3 Now explain that you are going to do the same thing, but this time listening instead of reading. Give some more instructions following the same format as the example above: *Let's meet at the corner of … and …* Ask learners to say which place you are referring to.

4 If the learners are failing to give the correct answer, focus on the pronunciation of the street names which are causing difficulty, paying attention to the differences between them. Do simple minimal pair activities with the problem words. For example, write on the board:
   A = *state,* **B** = *straight*
   Now say one of the words and ask learners to say if it is **A** or **B**.

Follow up

Put learners in pairs or groups for them to play the game together. One of them gives directions and the other(s) have to identify the correct place. Although we are using this activity in this book to focus on the listening skill, it's also useful for learners to try to produce the different consonant clusters as this will make them more aware of the problem.

Cluster Maps
Map 1

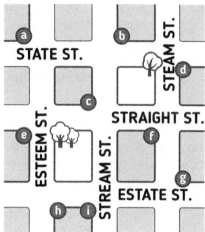

Map 2

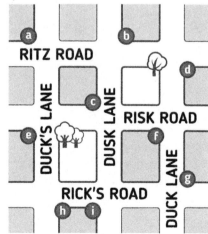

B3 Land of lost letters

This activity aims to raise awareness of silent letters. These consonants which are not pronounced can cause listening difficulties if the learner expects to hear them.

Background
Many English spellings contain consonant letters which were once part of the pronunciation of the word but which are no longer pronounced. Often, a learner's first experience of a new word is in the written form, and they form a mistaken mental record of how it's pronounced. As a result, they may fail to recognise the word while listening. It is worth raising awareness of these significant differences between the sound and the spelling.

The activity
The materials for this activity include a map and a short story. The main towns on the map (in bold below) each contain a silent letter, and in the region around the main town, all the villages have names with the same silent letter.

Knoxville (Silent K): <u>knee</u>, <u>knock</u>, know, <u>knife</u>
Point of Honour (Silent H): honest, <u>hour</u>, heir, <u>ghost</u>
Tombstone (Silent B): lamb, <u>comb</u>, <u>thumb</u>, <u>climb</u>, debt, <u>doubt</u>
Autumn Lake (Silent N): column, condemn
Half Way House (Silent L): <u>walk</u>, <u>could</u>, <u>calm</u>, folk, yolk, chalk
Small Isle (Silent S): <u>island</u>, <u>debris</u>, aisle
Brighton (Silent GH): <u>lighthouse</u>, eight, thought
Wrexham (Silent W): wrap, wrist, <u>write</u>, two, who
Sovereign City (Silent G): design, <u>sign</u>
Newcastle (Silent T): Christmas, <u>fasten</u>, whistle, <u>listen</u>

Map
Give out or display the map for the class. To get them familiar with it, call out the names of each main town and ask the class to reply by calling out the names of the villages around it. Ask them to identify which silent letter the main town and surrounding villages have in common. Also, if there are any common patterns, draw learner's attention to them – for example, the silent K appears before an 'n' at the beginning of a word.

▶ Story
Tell the learners they will hear a story which contains many of the words on the map. Ask them to underline (or make a note of) all of the words they hear while listening (they are underlined in the list above). Then read out the story [or ▶ play audio B3].

Optional follow up

Ask learners to remember as much of the story as they can. They could try to reconstruct the story cooperatively.

LAND OF LOST LETTERS

Story: The Ghost in the Lighthouse

There's an old lighthouse on the island and people talk about seeing a ghost in there. You can actually walk to the island at low tide, so we thought we'd go and take a look. After about half an hour, we arrived. I took a photo of Frank standing in front of the lighthouse smiling and making a thumbs-up gesture.

There was a chain on the door but it wasn't fastened. We opened the door and asked if anyone was there, but nobody answered of course. We climbed the stairs to the top and wrote our names in the dust on the glass. It was a calm autumn day and we sat and listened to the sound of the waves and the birds.

The inside of the lighthouse was full of debris, but you could still see the places where the old keeper used to sleep and cook. There was still a knife and fork on the table, and a comb as well. On our way back from the island, the tide was coming in and the water came up to our knees.

Back at home, I looked at the photo I took of Frank and noticed something very strange in the background. I don't believe in ghosts, but there was no doubt about it: there was the shadowy figure of a man standing at the top of the lighthouse!

PronPack: Word Recognition for Listeners

B4 Syllable Tennis

This activity aims to help learners to pay close attention to the syllables in words. Recognising common syllables in English is a key skill for learners to acquire.

Background

Most two-syllable nouns have the stress pattern **Oo** (the stress on the 1st syllable), and the words in this activity all have that pattern. Expert listeners often use syllables, especially stressed syllables, to help them recognise the word, and learners can be encouraged to do the same. This game is designed to focus learner attention on the syllables which comprise the words.

Syllable tennis

Sometimes, different words may share the same syllable. For example, *princess* and *printer* have the same first syllable; *printer* and *painter* have the same second syllable. In this game, learners 'hit' words back and forth like the ball in a game of tennis. When a player 'receives' a word from the other player, they must 'return' another word which with one syllable the same.

The game

Here, there are two versions of the game. You could use the first one for practice, going through the stages together as a whole class to show them how it works. Then you can leave them to do the second game separately in their pairs.

1 Put the class into pairs. In each pair, give one learner the instructions and word box for **Student A**. Give the other the instructions and word box for **Student B**. They should not be able to see each other's words.

2 Student **A** begins by calling out the start word (*habit* in **Game 1**, *message* in **Game 2**).

3 Student **B** listens to **A**'s word, finds a word with the same 2nd syllable in his/her word box and calls it out (*exit* in **Game 1**, *image* in **Game 2**).

4 Student **A** listens to **B**'s word, finds a word with the same 1st syllable in his/her word box and calls it out (*excess* in **Game 1**, *import* in **Game 2**).

5 They continue until all of the words have been used. The last word will be *bedroom* in **Game 1** or *pension* in **Game 2**.

6 Once they have completed the game, ask the pairs of learners to do it again a few times, getting faster each time, and remembering to always stress the first syllable.

Game 1

Student A: You start, using the word '**habit**'. After your partner responds, say a word from the box which has the *same first syllable* as your partner's word. All the words are nouns, with the stress pattern **Oo**.

A: Habit!... **B:** Exit!

A: ...

> habit, actor, classroom, comic, excess, moment, painting, printer

---

Student B: Say a word from the box which has the *same last syllable* as your partner's word. When you reach the word '**bedroom**', you have finished the game. All the words are nouns, with the stress pattern **Oo**.

A: Habit! ... **B:** Exit! ...

A: Excess ... **B:** ...

> acting, classic, comment, exit, motor, painter, princess, bedroom

Game 2

Student A: You start, using the word '**message**'. After your partner responds, say a word from the box which has the *same first syllable* as your partner's word. All the words are nouns, with the stress pattern **Oo**.

A: Message! ... **B:** Image!

A: ...

> message, action, contest, extract, fusion, import, nature, process

---

Student B: Say a word from the box which has the same last syllable as your partner's word. When you reach the word 'pension', you have finished the game. All the words are nouns, with the stress pattern **Oo**.

A: Message! ... **B:** Image! ...

A: import! ... **B:** ...

> access, contract, export, future, image, nation, protest, pension

Follow up

Give or show learners the 'syllable ladder'. This is a written version of the syllable tennis game. The nouns are printed, but most of the 1st syllables are missing. Learners have to look in the box of 1st syllables and find the correct one to write in each gap in the ladder. They can do this partly by remembering the words from the syllable tennis game, or else just by puzzling it out.

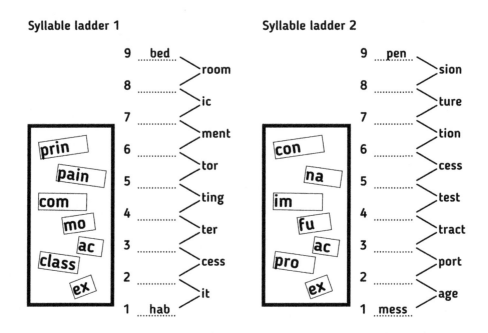

Syllable ladder 1

Syllable ladder 2

Key for Ladder 1:

    2 - *ex*, **3** - *prin*, **4** - *pain*, **5** - *ac*, **6** - *mo*, **7** - *com*, **8** - *class*

Key for Ladder 2:

    2 - *im*, **3** - *ex*, **4** - *con*, **5** - *pro*, **6** - *ac*, **7** - *na*, **8** - *fu*

B5 Flipping Syllables

This activity aims to help learners to pay close attention to the syllables in words. Recognising common syllables in English is a key skill for learners to acquire.

Background

There is a form of slang in French called 'verlan', in which the order of syllables in a word is reversed or 'flipped'. For example, the word like *weekend* – if we 'flip' the order of the syllables, it becomes *endweek*. This kind of word-play could be used in English to help learners become more familiar with the concept of syllables. To keep things simple, we will focus on words of only two syllables.

Flipping is easiest where words are compounds – for example, if you flip *football* you get *ballfoot*. Other words are slightly less obvious – for example *joyen* for *enjoy*. Bear in mind that a some words may be difficult or impossible to flip, for example *little*.

The game

1 Using the example of *football* and *ballfoot*, explain the concept of flipping syllables to the class.

2 Now call out flipped words such as the examples below. Learners listen and try to call back the correct word, for example:

You: *daybirth!*

Learner: *birthday!*

daybirth = birthday; byegood = goodbye; endweek = weekend; onesome = someone; teensix = sixteen; nicpic = picnic; fastbreak = breakfast; phonesmart = smartphone; siteweb = website; shopbook = bookshop

Note: You should try to pronounce the flipped syllables in the same way as the syllables in the correct word. For example, say fastbreak like this: /fəstˈbrek/.

3 If you want to make it easier, give the learners a word bank with the correct answers jumbled:

birthday, goodbye, weekend, breakfast, picnic, someone, smartphone, bookshop, website, sixteen

4 You could make the game more challenging by introducing two-word phrases such as the examples below:

Daysun ningeve = Sunday evening; Daymon ningmor = Monday morning; bernum ensev = number seven; toplap boardkey = laptop keyboard; drenchil ingplay = children playing; joyen selfyour = enjoy yourself; Donlon itax = London taxi; engard ypart = garden party

5 Learners may enjoy creating their own flipped words, which they can then read aloud for their classmates to 'translate' back into normal English. Advise them to use 2-syllable words. Bear in mind that some words can't be easily flipped, however – for example *little*.

▶ Follow up

Tell learners that you will read out a story which is full of flipped-syllable words. Then read out the story below [or ▶ play audio B5] and ask learners to listen and try to explain what happened in the story.

Last endweek, I got up on Daysun ningmor and had a cup of eecoff. I had some fastbreak, looked at my toplap and read the lineshead on a news siteweb. Then I went sideout for a walk. It was zingfree cold but the shinesun was lylove. As I was ingstand by the lake, I heard a 'ping' on my phonesmart. It was a new agemess from my old friendgirl. It said 'Sorry I gotfor your daybirth!'. 'No lemprob', I pliedre 'It's next Daythurs!'.

B6 Crossverbs puzzle

This activity aims to familiarise learners with some common unstressed syllables at the start of English words.

Background

A majority of two-syllable verbs have the stress pattern oO (the stress on the 2nd syllable). The opening syllable, which is unstressed, usually contains a reduced, weak vowel – /ə/ or /ɪ/ and may be hard for a listener to hear clearly. Since there are a limited number of such syllables in English, it's worth helping learners to become more accustomed to hearing them.

The game

1 Give out the Crossverb puzzle, or show it to the learners on screen.

2 Explain that they must fill in gaps **1–8** with the missing syllables (shown below the puzzle). All of the words are verbs with two syllables. Stressed syllables are given in capitals.

3 Go through the example with the class. Point out that it forms a word in both directions – horizontally and vertically, making the words control and confuse.

CROSSVERBS PUZZLE

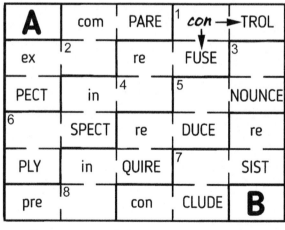

Answers: **1** = *con*, **2** = *PLAIN*, **3** = *an*, **4** = *SULT*, **5** = *pro*, **6** = *re*, **7** = *in*, **8** = *TEND*

PronPack: Word Recognition for Listeners

▶ Listening activity

Ask the learners to use the completed puzzle in an audio maze activity to familiarise them with the sound of these verbs in context. Point out that you can get from **A** to **B** on the puzzle by crossing a set of four verbs (for example, expect – insult – produce – insist). Tell them they will hear some very short stories. For each story, they must listen for the verbs and find the correct path from **A** to **B**. Now read out one or more of the stories below [or ▶ play audio B6]. After each story, check the answers (given in brackets).

A to B stories

1 She was a difficult customer. She complained about the starter and refused to eat it. But when I announced that the desert was on the house, she couldn't resist ordering the apple pie.
(***Answer:* A** – *complain – refuse – announce – resist* – **B**)

2 Martin's very impatient. When he sends an email, he expects you to reply immediately. You can pretend you're busy, but he'll simply conclude that you're lazy or rude, or both!
(***Answer:* A** – *expect – reply – pretend – conclude* – **B**)

3 People always try to compare Jenny and Kate. They're identical twins, and it's easy to confuse them. The only difference is the way they pronounce the word 'scone'. Kate tells Jenny it should rhyme with 'stone', but Jenny resists and makes it rhyme with 'gone'.
(***Answer:* A** – *compare – confuse – pronounce – resist* – **B**)

4 The head teacher got Paul into the office and asked him to explain why he'd hit Brian. 'He insulted me', said Paul. 'It's not good enough', said the head, 'I think Brian requires an apology, and I insist that you do it immediately!'
(***Answer:* A** – *explain – insult – require – insist* – **B**)

Follow up

Learners could work in pairs or small groups and try to retell the **A** to **B** stories from memory. Alternatively, they could invent stories of their own using verbs on a path from **A** to **B**.

B7 Schwa Riddles

The weak vowel schwa can be difficult for listeners to hear, and different from the vowel they expect from the spelling. It is one of the main challenges in listening to English.

. . . .

Background

In an unstressed syllable, the vowel is often reduced to the weak sound known as schwa (represented by the symbol /ə/). This happens in the second syllable of word **1** below. This vowel reduction doesn't always happen though. In word **2**, the second syllable has the full vowel /eɪ/, as you would expect from the spelling.

1 *climate* /ə/

2 *flatmate* /eɪ/

The schwa sound may cause difficulties for learner listeners, firstly because it's hard to hear, and secondly because it is not what they would expect from the spelling. For the benefit of listening, then, it's worth focusing on vowel reduction in class.

▶ Raise awareness

Show learners the earworm below and read it out for them [or ▶ play audio B7]. Read out the text line by line, inviting them to repeat. Check they are keeping the same rhythm. Make sure you reduce the vowel to schwa in the last syllable of each line. Check the learners understand the meaning of each line refers to the pronunciation: *mate* in *climate* is not pronounced the same as *mate* on its own. The vowel in *mate* sounds like the letter **A** in the alphabet, but the second vowel in *climate* is a very short and weak sound. You could do this drill a few times until learners get used to it. Follow up with one or more of the activities below.

There's no 'late' in 'chocolate'
And no 'mate' in 'climate'

There's no 'met' in 'helmet'
And no 'let' in 'toilet

There's no 'lot' in 'pilot'
And no 'rot' in 'parrot'

There's no 'board' in 'cupboard'
There's no 'ward' in 'forward'

The riddles

1 Write the following riddle on the board and ask learners for the answer. Explain that the answer is a short word of just one syllable.
It's in 'unless' but not in 'useless'. *(**Answer:** less)*

2 Elicit an explanation of the riddle. *(**Answer:** both words contain the sequence of letters l-e-s-s. The sequence is pronounced like 'less' in 'unless', but in 'useless' it isn't because the vowel is reduced to a schwa.)*

3 Now explain that you will read out some more similar riddles and ask learners to call out the answer as quickly as possible. Choose riddles from the list below.

Schwa Riddles

1 It's in 'passport' but not in 'compass'. *(**Answer:** pass)*

2 It's in 'tennis' but not in 'written'. *(**Answer:** ten)*

3 It's in 'apple' but not in 'apply'. *(**Answer:** app)*

4 It's in 'centre' but not in 'recent'. *(**Answer:** cent)*

5 It's in 'carpet' but not in 'career'. *(**Answer:** car)*

6 It's in 'bandage' but not in 'banana'. *(**Answer:** ban)*

7 It's in 'Spiderman' but not in 'woman'. (***Answer:** man)*

8 It's in 'football' but not in 'balloon'. *(**Answer:** ball)*

9 It's in 'forty' but not in 'comfort'. *(**Answer:** fort)*

10 It's in 'celebrate' but not in 'pirate'. *(**Answer:** rate)*

11 It's in 'pencil' but not in 'open'. *(**Answer:** pen)*

12 It's in 'suppose' but not in 'purpose'. *(**Answer:** pose)*

Alternative procedures

– Learners write their answers to the riddles and then check the answers at the end.

– Put learners in teams. The first team to answer each riddle wins a point.

B8 Stepping Stones

This activity aims to familiarize learners with how longer words are broken down into a number of syllables.

Background

In pronunciation teaching, we often think of individual sounds as being the building blocks of words. However, there is a bigger unit – the syllable – which possibly plays a more significant role in spoken word recognition. Learner listeners will benefit from becoming more familiar with how longer words break down into syllables, and this activity should help. For the purposes of designing games like this, it has been necessary to decide how exactly to separate the syllables and the principles we have used for doing this are outlined in **Tip A7**.

The game

There are two versions of this game. The first is smaller and focuses on 3-syllable words. The second is larger and focuses on 4-syllable words. The ovals in the game represent stepping stones in a river, and there is one syllable written on each stone.

1 Give out the game, or show it to learners on screen. Explain that they must join syllables to find words which go across the 'river' from left to right. Go through the example given (*potato* version 1, *celebration* in version 2).

2 Tell learners to find more words in the game. While they are doing this, you should warn them that some 'stones' are used in more than one word.

3 As you go through the correct answers together, you could ask learners to identify the stressed syllable in each of the words. These are underlined in the answer keys.

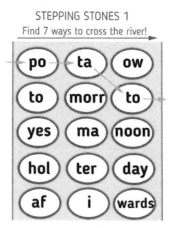

STEPPING STONES 1
Find 7 ways to cross the river!

(**Answers:** *potato, tomorrow, tomato, yesterday, holiday, afternoon, afterwards*)

STEPPING STONES 2
Find 8 ways to cross the river!

(**Answers:** *celebration, environment, entertainment, alternative, certificate, intelligence, information, calculation*)

B9 Syllable Soup

This activity aims to familiarize learners with how longer words can be divided into syllables, and how one of these is stressed.

Background

Learner listeners will benefit from becoming more familiar with the idea of syllables, and how these are like the building blocks of words. This activity is intended to make syllables more noticeable to the learners. For the purposes of designing games like this, it has been necessary to decide how exactly to separate the syllables and the principles we have used for doing this are outlined in **Tip A7**.

The game

1 Give out the game, or show it to learners on screen. Explain that they have to find words in the grid. Each word has three syllables (and each square contains a syllable). The squares can be joined horizontally, diagonally or vertically.

2 There are a total of 15 words in the soup, and one of them is given as an example. The stressed syllable of each of the words is given in a numbered list next to the grid. Learners should outline the words that they find, and underline the stressed syllable. They could also tick off the stressed syllables **1–15** as they find them.

3 As you go through the correct answers together, ask learners to practice saying the words, using the correct stress.

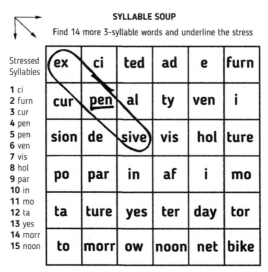

SYLLABLE SOUP

Find 14 more 3-syllable words and underline the stress

Stressed Syllables					
ex	ci	ted	ad	e	furn
cur	pen	al	ty	ven	i
sion	de	sive	vis	hol	ture
po	par	in	af	i	mo
ta	ture	yes	ter	day	tor
to	morr	ow	noon	net	bike

Stressed Syllables

1 ci
2 furn
3 cur
4 pen
5 pen
6 ven
7 vis
8 hol
9 par
10 in
11 mo
12 ta
13 yes
14 morr
15 noon

(*Answers:* **1** – excited, **2** furniture, **3** – excursion, **4** – expensive, **5** – penalty, **6** – adventure, **7** – visitor, **8** – holiday, **9** – departure, **10** – internet, **11** – motorbike, **12** – potato, **13** – yesterday, **14** – tomorrow, **15** – afternoon)

B10 Syllable Spotting

This activity aims to show learners that paying attention to stressed syllables is a key strategy in listening.

Background

Word stress plays an important role in helping listeners to recognise words. In the case of English, when listeners hear a stressed syllable, they know it is most likely the beginning of a new word. That's because if you add all of the one-syllable content words together with other content words with stress on the first syllable, you have over 90% of the content words of the language. Using word stress as a guide to word-recognition is a useful strategy for learners to acquire.

Awareness-raising activity

Show learners the sentences below. Say the sentences and get the class to repeat. Do this two or three times. Point out that each sentence has nine syllables, but only three of them are stressed – the first syllable of each word. The stress pattern is this:
Ooo Ooo Ooo

> **Foot**ballers **cel**ebrate **pen**alties.
>
> **Grand**parents **ed**ucate **teen**agers.
>
> **Trav**ellers **org**anise **hol**idays.
>
> **Journ**alists **int**erview **wit**nesses.
>
> **Com**panies **ad**vertise **serv**ices.

Now stop showing the sentences, or ask learners not to look at them. Say the sentences, but only the stressed syllables. Ask learners to say what the complete sentence was, from memory. For example:

You: *Trav – org – hol.*

Learners: *Travellers organise holidays!*

▶ Listening activity

The sentences in this activity contain multiple instances of the same stressed syllable. Learners listen and identify the syllable which they hear at least three times. For this activity, it's not essential that the learners are familiar with all of the words in the sentences.

1 Give learners the jumbled answers, which is a list of syllables: *an, con, em, en, ex, gen, in, min, pen, pre, re, sat.* Explain that they will hear a sentence which contains one of these syllables many times (at least three).

2 Read out the sentences [or ▶ play audio B10]. Learners listen and underline each of the syllables in the jumbled answer list as they hear them.

3 Say (or play) the sentences again. Stop after each one and ask learners to say the repeated syllable. They could also say the whole words which the syllables came from, if they can remember them.

4 Check the answers. You could allow them to read the sentences at this point, on screen or on a print-out.

To make this activity more difficult, don't give learners the list of jumbled answers. Instead, they listen and make a note of the repeated syllable in each sentence.

1 The pensioner got a pencil, drew a penguin and sold it for a penny. *(Answer: pen)*

2 The old general was generally a generous gentleman. *(Answer: gen)*

3 Finding the exit is an excellent way of getting extra exercise. *(Answer: ex)*

4 We'll use all our energy to stop enemies from entering. *(Answer: en)*

5 It was hard to concentrate on the concert after the conference. *(Answer: con)*

6 Andrew answered questions about animals in the Andes. *(Answer: an)*

7 Students at the institute were interviewed about the incident. *(Answer: in)*

8 The minister had a mineral water ten minutes ago. *(Answer: min)*

9 I'm satisfied after seeing a satellite on Saturday. *(Answer: sat)*

10 Our emphasis is on getting the emeralds out of the embassy. *(Answer: em)*

11 I've seen all the recent research about retail in the region. *(Answer: re)*

12 We paid a premium to preview the previous episodes. *(Answer: pre)*

Jumbled answers: an, con, em, en, ex, gen, in, min, pen, pre, re, sat.

B11 Lost Middles Maze

This activity aims to raise learner awareness of syllable elision. This frequently happens to weak middle syllables in longer words.

Background

When a syllable is unstressed, the vowel is often reduced to a schwa /ə/, or sometimes /ɪ/. The amount of reduction varies between speakers and occasions, but in the most extreme case the vowel may be lost altogether. As a consequence, an entire syllable may be lost. For example, the middle vowel in the word *family* may be lost so that the word has only two syllables, sounding like this: *famly*. The most common place for this kind of syllable elision is in the middle of a word, as in the example, hence we may call this phenomenon 'lost middles'. It can be represented in the syllable diagram **Ooo** (big circle = stressed syllable, small circles = weak syllables). The letter following the lost middle is usually '**r**', '**l**' or '**n**', as in these examples:

> **r:** camera, memory
>
> **l:** family, chocolate
>
> **n:** listening, national

However, there are some other examples where the elision happens before other consonants: vegetable, comfortable, medicine.

Awareness-raising activity

Show learners these three words: **a.** *hamburger*, **b.** *omelette*, **c.** *chocolate*

Say the words out loud, making sure you don't pronounce the first 'e' in *omelette* or the second 'o' in *chocolate*. Ask learners to count the syllables in each word. Elicit that *hamburger* has three, but the others have only two – the middle syllable is cut. Introduce the term 'lost middles'.

Now show learners the groups of words below. Ask them to listen, and for each group they should say which word can <u>not</u> have a lost middle.

1. **a.** thundering, **b.** lightening, **c.** hurricane

2. **a.** factory, **b.** offices, **c.** nursery

3. **a.** gardener, **b.** prisoner, **c.** footballer

4. **a.** happening, **b.** promising, **c.** travelling

5. **a.** desperate, **b.** moderate, **c.** delicate

   (*Answers:* **1** – *c,* **2** *b,* **3** – *c,* **4** – *b,* **5** – *c*)

The game

Give learners a copy of the maze or project it on the screen. Explain that the objective is to find a route from top left to bottom right. They can only pass squares containing a word with a 'lost middle'. After going through the answers at the end, ask learners to look at the consonant letters which comes after the 'lost middles'. Point out that they are one of these: '**r**', '**l**' or '**n**'.

⬤⊗⬤	bicycle	camera	personal	memory
history	family	different	holiday	evening
anything	politics	quality	every	chocolate
listening	national	aspirin	favourite	animal
factory	elephant	article	customer	comedy
mystery	traveller	opening	general	⬤⊗⬤

(**Answers:** history, family, different, camera, personal, memory, evening, chocolate, every, favourite, aspirin, national, listening, factory, mystery, traveller, opening, general)

▶ Follow up listening activity

Read out the following story [or ▶ play audio B11]. Ask learners to listen and notice any words with 'lost middles'. Then they can listen a second time with the script in front of them and underline the words.

One ordinary evening, my family and I were sitting in our comfortable living room, listening to my favourite music and enjoying some chocolate. My brother was looking through the photos on his personal camera when he paused on a strange one. "What is this?" he asked, showing us the photo. It was a picture of our living room, but in the corner was someone that none of us knew. We couldn't think of anyone who it could be. We spent the rest of the day trying to solve the mystery, but we never did find out the truth. It remains a strange memory from that otherwise ordinary day

(**Answers:** ordinary, evening, family, comfortable, listening, favourite, chocolate, personal, camera, mystery, memory)

B12 Trictation

This activity aims to raise learner awareness of the difficulty of word boundary recognition, and encourage them to listen flexibly, modifying their first understandings when necessary.

Background
In spoken English, unexpected homophones sometimes occur. For example, the two phrases below sound exactly the same: the listener cannot tell which one they are hearing until they hear more of the context.

   a. *the dresses*

   b. *the dress is*

Listeners must be flexible. For example, you may think you heard a. above, but then the speaker continues with the word 'nice'. Now, option a. no longer makes sense, and you have to change your interpretation to b. Learner listeners are often not flexible in this way, sticking to their first interpretation and getting lost as a result.

Word boundary recognition
The example above demonstrates how difficult word boundary recognition is: the listener has to decide if they're hearing one word – *dresses* or two words – *dress is*. Sometimes it's impossible to know to begin with, and you have to revise your interpretation as you continue to listen. The activity in this lesson aims to give learners intensive practice in revising their interpretations, in order to become more flexible as listeners. It's a form of dictation which deliberately misleads the listener to begin with.

Trictation: dictation with a trick
Trictation is a form of dictation in two steps. First, you read out the beginning of a phrase (for example, *the dress is…*) and the learners write it down. Then you read out the full phrase – beginning and ending (for example, *the dress is nice*) – and they complete it. This will almost certainly involve correcting what they wrote in the first step (for instance, in step 1 of the example above, they are likely to think you said *the dresses*).

▶ The game
1 Tell learners they will hear a short phrase. Ask them to write down what they hear. Then read out part **a.** from the first sentence below [or ▶ play audio B12].

2 Tell learners they will hear the phrase again with a bit more so they can complete it. Tell them to write the complete sentence. Then read out part **b.** (or use the audio).

3 Ask learners if they wrote the first part of the sentence correctly at **step 1** – and if not, why not? You should assure them that if they got the first part wrong, it wasn't their fault – the beginning of the sentence has more than one possible understanding.

4 Continue with the rest of the sentences.

1	**a.** the dresses	**b.** the dress is nice
2	**a.** a long wait	**b.** a long way to go
3	**a.** they talked	**b.** they talk too much
4	**a.** whose picture	**b.** who's picked your apples?
5	**a.** the oranges	**b.** the orange is delicious!
6	**a.** watch	**b.** what's your name?

▶ Follow up

It is probably a good idea to do this activity a few times so that learners really get used to the idea. Below are two more collections of 'trictation' sentences you could use [or ▶ play audio].

The schwa collection

The schwa is sometimes involved in problems of word-boundary recognition: it's hard to know which word it belongs with, and listeners may have to modify their interpretation as they hear more.

1	**a.** A newer dish	**b.** A new edition.
2	**a.** Antwerp's a port	**b.** Antwerp supporters.
3	**a.** Got up at eight	**b.** Got a potato salad.
4	**a.** Here's my pencil	**b.** Here's my pen selection.
5	**a.** It's a fish	**b.** It's official.
6	**a.** That's a mess	**b.** That semester.
7	**a.** We kept the petal	**b.** We kept the pet alive.
8	**a.** What's Europe	**b.** What's your opinion?
9	**a.** You've got a point	**b.** You've got appointments.

The consonant cluster collection

Consonant clusters sometimes involved in problems of word-boundary recognition: it's hard to know which word a consonant belongs with, and listeners may have to modify their interpretation as they hear more.

1	**a.** it snows	**b.** its nose is wet
2	**a.** my aunt's old	**b.** my aunt sold her car
3	**a.** Juliet's lips	**b.** Juliet slips on the ice
4	**a.** that's low	**b.** that slow lorry
5	**a.** the boy in short sleeves	**b.** the boy in shorts leaves early
6	**a.** the parrot speaks	**b.** the parrot's beak's yellow
7	**a.** Albert stays	**b.** Albert's days are over
8	**a.** the laptop screen	**b.** the laptop's green and black
9	**a.** The ship's in port	**b.** The ship's important.

Section C Lexis for listeners

In this section, you will find 18 lessons, each focusing on words with specific beginnings or endings.

Lexis provides a natural organising principle for lessons which focus on spoken word recognition. There are certain syllables which are frequently found at the start or end of words, and familiarity with these can help learners to listen more fluently. Each lesson in this section focuses on one or more of these word segments. For each lesson, there are various activities to choose from – you don't have to use them all. They can be used as stand-alone lessons, or integrated into lessons with a focus on vocabulary.

Audio files

All of the lessons have audio files available for any activities which are indicated by the symbol ►. These can be downloaded from the **Resources** section for this book on the PronPack website.

Worksheets

For any of the activities which require handouts or slides to share with your learners, these are available and downloadable from the **Resources** section for this book on the PronPack website. There are colour slides available for all of the short rhymes labelled *Earworm*.

C1 Word endings *er, or, ar, our, re*

The word endings *-er, -or, -ar, -our, -re*

▶ **Earworm**

Neighbours

I'm your **neighb**our
Mister **Fraz**er
Do me a **fav**our
Lend me a **shav**er

Here's a **raz**or
Mister **Fraz**er
Call me **Iv**or
Lend me a **fiv**er?

Words with endings *er, or, ar, our, re*

The word endings *er, or, ar, our* and *re* are very common in English, and they may all sound identical when the syllable is unstressed. Here are some examples:

er: *walker, teacher, cooker, bigger, caller, winner, father, sister, supper, water, Peter*

or: *sailor, actor, doctor, elevator, Victor, error, razor*

ar: *sugar, collar, dollar, Oscar*

UK *our* or US *or*: *flavour, colour, glamour, labour, rumour, neighbour*

UK *re* or US *er*: *centre, litre, metre*

Word recognition difficulty

The word endings *er, or, ar, our* and *re* are all pronounced the same – either /ə/, or /ər/. Learners may find these difficult to identify for two reasons:

1 They are very weak because the vowel sound is reduced to /ə/ (schwa).

2 The pronunciation does not reflect the spelling – there are many different vowel letters all reduced to the same vowel sound.

Failure to correctly identify this syllable can lead to difficulty in recognising the whole word.

Note: There are a few words with these endings which do not usually have a reduced vowel, for example *corridor, contour, mentor*. In a few words, these endings are stressed, for example *cigar, prefer*.

Raise awareness

Show learners the earworm (you may prefer to give them the version with the American spellings *neighbor* and *favor*) and read it out for them [or ▶ play audio C1]. Read out the text line by line, inviting them to repeat keeping the same rhythm. Try to include a weak vowel in the word endings *er, or* and *our*. Ask learners to guess the meaning of *fiver* (it's a five-pound or five-dollar note). Elicit a response from the learners to the situation in the poem, for example:

> Where's the speaker?
> Will the neighbour give them what they ask for?
> What would YOU do if you were in this situation?

Ask learners to find three rhyming pairs words in the earworm. When you check the answers, point out how the endings sound the same even though the spelling is different.

> (**Answers:** *favour – shaver; Frazer – razor; Ivor – fiver*)

Match the rhyming words

Ask learners to match rhyming words from list **A** and list **B**. Rhyming words are pronounced the same from the stressed vowel until the end of the word, for example, the underlined sections in this pair: s<u>weeter</u> – m<u>etre</u>

A *sweeter, saver, barber, liquor, cuter, sailor, flyer, motor, dancer, centre*

B *flavour, harbour, answer, enter, liar, metre, paler, quicker, tutor, voter*

> (**Answers:** *sweeter – metre, saver – flavour, barber – harbour, liquor – quicker, cuter – tutor, sailor – paler, flyer – liar, motor – voter, dancer – answer, centre – enter*)

▶ Do a listening exercise

Read out the phone messages below [or ▶ play audio] and ask learners to make a note of the most important information. Ask them to compare their answers with a partner to see if they have the same information.

> ***First message:*** Hello, this is Oscar Peters speaking, from Paper Tiger, the print shop, just to say your colour posters are ready to be collected.

> ***Second message:*** Hi, this is Heather from the Health Centre, just to remind you about your appointment with Doctor O'Connor at two thirty on Friday.

> ***Third message:*** Hi, Victor speaking from Silver Scissors, the barbers, just to let you know you left your wallet in the shop this morning.

C2 Word ending *ate*

The suffix *-ate* in adjectives, nouns and verbs

▶ Earworm

Chocolate

Chocolate's **great**
To **celebrate**
To **mo**tivate
To **decorate**

But **don't** put **choco**late
In an **ome**lette
That's just **des**perate
Keep them **sep**arate

Words ending *ate*

The ending *ate* in verbs like *locate* or *celebrate* has a full vowel /eɪt/. Meanwhile, in adjectives like *desperate* and nouns like *chocolate*, the vowel in ate becomes a schwa: /ət/. Words like *separate*, which are both verb and adjective, have two pronunciations, one with /eɪt/ and the other with /ət/. Many words with the ending *ate* are quite high-level, so some of the activities below are not suitable for lower level learners.

Word recognition difficulty

The *ate* ending can be problematic when it has a reduced vowel, as in the case of adjectives like *desperate* and nouns like *chocolate*. Not only is it hard to hear, but also learners may expect a longer vowel because of the spelling, with that final 'magic' 'e'. Recognising words like *separate*, *desperate* and *chocolate* is made even more difficult because the middle syllable may be cut ('lost middles' – see **B11**). As a result, separate may sound something like **seprut*.

Raise awareness

Show learners the earworm and read it out for them line by line [or ▶ play audio C2]. Alternatively, learners may 'play' the text using text-to-speech software such as is available in Microsoft Word. Make sure that learners notice the pronunciation of these words in the second verse: *chocolate*; *omelette*, *desperate*, *separate*. In all of them, the middle vowel sound is cut, and the final vowel sound is the weak vowel schwa.

Elicit a response from the learners to the situation in the poem, for example:

What is chocolate good for?
What is it not good for?
Do you agree?

▶ Find the odd-one-out

Show the class the following groups of words. Ask learners to look at the words in each list and decide which one has a different final syllable. Then read out the words [or ▶ play audio] for them to check their answers.

1 chocolate, omelette, pilot, calculate

2 carrot, favourite, decorate, desperate

3 delicate, locate, educate, complicate

4 automate, climate, helmet, ultimate

5 fortunate, fascinate, infinite, passionate

6 activate, motivate, private, innovate

   (**Answers: 1** *calculate,* **2** *decorate,* **3** *delicate,* **4** *automate,* **5** *fascinate,* **6** *private*)

▶ Is it a verb?

Show the class the table below and demonstrate the difference in pronunciation between the verbs and the adjective or noun. Point out that the verb has the ending /eɪt/ while the adjective or noun has the ending /ət/.

	graduate	**separate**
A (verb)	/grædjueɪt/	/sepəreɪt/
B (noun/adjective)	/grædjuət/	/seprət/

Now read out words from the list below [or ▶ play audio], pronounced either as a verb, or as an adjective or noun. After each word, learners should call out either **A** – verb or **B** – noun/adjective.

   graduate, separate, estimate, moderate, articulate, advocate, alternate, duplicate, animate, delegate, associate, coordinate, degenerate

As a follow up, show learners these sentences and ask them to try and pronounce them.

1 When did the graduate graduate?

2 Delegate to the delegates!

3 Don't associate with his associates.

4 People who aren't moderate can't moderate.

5 How did you estimate your estimate?

6 Alternate the work on alternate days.

Dictate expressions including words with *ate*

The expressions below consist of a word with *ate* followed by another word which collocates with it. Choose a few of them for a dictation exercise. Say each expression twice and ask learners to write what they hear. This involves learners being able to identify the word boundary in the phrases. Repeat the activity with several of the expressions.

climate change, moderate price, separate rooms, alternate days, accurate numbers, immediate effect, private beach, animate object, associate professor, delicate situation, chocolate box, favourite song, passionate kiss, ultimate challenge, fortunate circumstance

▶ Do a listening exercise

Read out the sentence below [or ▶ play audio] and ask learners to note all of the words they hear which end with *ate* (they are underlined). Ask them to compare their answers with a partner to see if they have the same words. Then check the answers.

A graduate's private research has provided a more accurate estimate of carbon emissions for separate households, which could have immediate impacts on the climate.

C3 Word endings *ory*, *ary* and *ery*

The adjective and noun endings *ory*, *ary* and *ery*

▶ **Earworm**

Work History
Worked in a **fact**ory
Did whatever **nec**essary
Got the job in **Jan**uary
Lost the job in **Feb**ruary

Worked as a **sec**retary
That was only **vol**untary
That's my work **hist**ory
The **fu**ture's still a **myst**ery

Words with endings *ory*, *ary* and *ery*
The endings *ory*, *ary* and *ery* are unstressed. The difference between 'a', or 'e' and 'o' is often neutralized so all three letters may represent the weak vowel /ə/. In fact, in many cases the vowel is not pronounced at all, so that the syllable is lost – for example, *history* may be pronounced as two syllables, with the 'o' cut altogether: /ˈhɪstrɪ/. This is part of a more general tendency for weak vowels to be cut before /r/.

Word recognition difficulty
Being unstressed, the endings ory, ary and ery are difficult to hear, but that is not the only problem; there is also a lot of variation in how they are pronounced. As mentioned above, many speakers cut the vowel sound before the 'r'. There is also accent variation in many of the words. For example, in *voluntary*, the 'a' in the ending is reduced to /ə/ or cut entirely in the UK, while in the US it is pronounced as a full vowel.

Raise awareness
Show learners the earworm and read it out for them [or ▶ play audio C3] – [there is also a rap version available]. Read out the text line by line, inviting them to repeat keeping the same rhythm.

If you are using the recording, point out the pronunciation of the endings *ory*, *ary* and *ery*: they are /ərɪ/ for gallery and salary, and just /rɪ/ for the rest. If you are reading it out yourself, your version of the endings *ory*, *ary* and *ery* may differ from the recording. Ask questions to focus on the meaning of the poem, for example:

Do you think the speaker enjoyed any of the jobs? Why / Why not?

Match beginnings and endings

Match the beginnings and endings to make words. Use each beginning once. Then practice saying the words.

Beginnings: *anni, dic, voc, lib, ord, del, lav, pri*

Endings: *abulary, atory, inary, ivery, mary, rary, tionary , versary*

> (**Answers:** *anniversary, dictionary, vocabulary, library, ordinary, delivery, lavatory, primary*)

Guess the spelling

When note-taking, listeners will often have to write down words they haven't heard before, guessing the spelling from the sound. To develop this skill, you could dictate some invented words such as the examples below. Then ask learners to compare their spellings with a partner.

> *appellery, fanastory, sillary, mangatory*

▶ Do a listening exercise

Read out the following news report [or ▶ play audio] and ask learners to listen and spot the word endings *ory*, *ary* and *ery* (they are <u>underlined</u>). You could organize this activity in different ways:

- ask learners to count the number of times they hear a word with these endings
- raise a hand each time they hear a word with one of the endings
- do the activity in teams, first listening for words with the endings and after, trying to remember as many of them as possible
- ask learners to listen and make notes. Then they summarise the story from their notes.

> Police are investigating a <u>robbery</u> at a <u>gallery</u> in the city. The thieves got away with a painting by Leonardo da Vinci which had been in a <u>temporary</u> exhibition in the <u>gallery</u> since <u>February</u>. It appears that the thieves hid in a <u>lavatory</u> until night and escaped in a <u>delivery</u> van. The location of the painting is still a <u>mystery</u> but police say they will do everything <u>necessary</u> to recover it safely.

C4 Word endings *ic* and *ical*

The adjective and noun suffixes *ic* and *ical*

▶ **Earworm**

Plastic

The **wat**er's full of **plast**ic
The **sit**uation's **drast**ic
Look at the Pa**cif**ic
The **facts** are scien**tif**ic
Call me pessi**mist**ic
I **think** I'm rea**list**ic
The **prob**lem's oce**an**ic
I **think** it's time to **pan**ic

Words with endings *ic* and *ical*

When listeners hear one of the the common adjective and noun endings *ic* and *ical*, they can be fairly confident that it is the end of a word, although there may be another suffix after it – for example, *basically*. The *ic* is pronounced as /ɪk/, and in *ical*, the final 'al' is /əl/, although the vowel may be inaudible.

A very noticeable feature of the adjective and noun endings *ic* and *ical* is that the main stress of the word will be on the syllable before, and this stressed syllable will have a strong vowel sound. This usually means that the pronunciation of that vowel will be different from the same vowel in the root word. For example, compare **o**cean and *oceanic*. In the first, the vowel pair 'ea' combine to make the weak vowel /ə/ but in the second the pair splits into two vowel sounds: /ɪ/ followed by the strong vowel /æ/.

Note: There are a few exceptions to the stress pattern – for example, in **A**rabic, the stress is 2 syllables before the *ic* ending.

Raise awareness

Show learners the earworm and read it out for them [or ▶ play audio C4] – [there is also a rap version available]. Read out the text line by line, inviting them to repeat keeping the same rhythm. Make sure that the stress is on the syllable before the ic ending. Ask a few questions to focus on the meaning of the poem, for example:

Do you think the speaker is pessimistic or realistic?

Do you agree with their point of view?

Match the rhyming words

Match words from **A** with a rhyming word from **B**. Rhyming words are two words which sound the same from the last stressed vowel until the end. Then practice saying the words.

A: *democratic, traffic, topical, comical, panic, Pacific, Atlantic, plastic, athletic, realistic*

B: *dramatic, economical, fantastic, geographic, mechanic, romantic, scientific, statistic, sympathetic, tropical*

> (**Answers:** *democratic – dramatic, traffic – geographic, topical – tropical, comical – economical, panic – mechanic, Pacific – scientific, Atlantic – romantic, plastic – fantastic, athletic – sympathetic, realistic – statistic*)

Guess the spelling

When note-taking, listeners will often have to write down words they haven't heard before, guessing the spelling from the sound. To develop this skill, you could dictate some invented words such as the examples below. Then ask learners to compare their spellings with a partner.

> *connistic, infinetic, tutoric, darlactical*

▶ Do a listening exercise

Read out the following news report [or ▶ play audio]. and ask learners to listen and spot the word endings *ic* and *ical* (they are <u>underlined</u>). You could organize this activity in different ways:

- ask learners to count the number of times they hear a word with these endings
- raise a hand each time they hear a word with one of the endings
- do the activity in teams, first listening for words with the endings and after, trying to remember as many of them as possible
- ask learners to listen and make notes. Then they summarise the story from their notes.

> Planners say <u>electric</u> cars will help to reduce <u>toxic</u> air pollution, but the <u>traffic</u> will still be <u>problematic</u> in our towns and cities unless we make <u>drastic</u> improvements to our <u>public</u> transport systems. We also need to make buses and trains more <u>economical</u> to use, and more <u>hygienic</u> too – this is something people have been asking for since the <u>pandemic</u>.

C5 Word endings *ant*, *ent*, *ance* and *ence*

The suffixes *ant*, *ent*, *ance* and *ence*

▶ **Earworm**

Assessment
Competent, in**tell**igent
Work is always **ex**cellent
But **not** exactly **el**egant
As **grace**ful as an **el**ephant!

So **con**fidence, in**tell**igence
Plenty of ex**per**ience
Competence and ex**cell**ence
But **not** a lot of **el**egance

Words with endings *ant*, *ent*, *ance* and *ence*

The suffixes *ant*, *ent*, *ance* and *ence* are unstressed. The difference between 'a' and 'e' is neutralized so both letters represent the weak vowel /ə/.

The *ant* and *ent* endings appear in adjectives (*excellent*, *intelligent*, *competent*) and nouns (*accident*, *parent*, *elephant*).

The *ance* and *ence* endings appear in abstract nouns (*intelligence*, *experience*, *elegance*).

Word recognition difficulty

Being unstressed, with a reduced vowel, the endings *ant*, *ent*, *ance* and *ence* are difficult to hear, and the syllable before these endings also usually contains a reduced vowel, so that there are two hard-to-hear syllables together. In addition to that, the 't' at the end of *ant* and *ent* is often inaudible, especially if the following word begins with a consonant sound.

Raise awareness

Show learners the earworm and read it out for them [or ▶ play audio C5]. Read out the text line by line, inviting them to repeat keeping the same rhythm. Point out that the stress in all the *ant*, *ent*, *ance* and *ence* words is two syllables from the end.

Ask questions to focus on the meaning of the poem, for example:

Would you give this person a job?

What job would be good for this kind of person?

Guess the spelling

When note-taking, listeners will often have to write down words they haven't heard before, guessing the spelling from the sound. To develop this skill, you could dictate some invented words such as the examples below. Then ask learners to compare their spellings with a partner.

camberant, palavent, setifluence, allotience

▶ Do a listening exercise

Read out the following texts [or ▶ play audio] and ask learners to listen and spot the word endings (they are <u>underlined</u>). You could organize this activity in different ways:

- ask learners to count the number of times they hear a word with the endings
- raise a hand each time they hear a word with one of the endings
- do the activity in teams, first listening for words with the endings and after, trying to remember as many of them as possible

Words ending *ant* and *ent*

After the <u>accident</u>, the <u>patient</u> was in <u>urgent</u> need of <u>treatment</u>. Thanks to the <u>intelligent</u> and <u>competent</u> response on the part of the ambulance team and the <u>convenient</u> location of a hospital, the <u>patient</u> received prompt attention and doctors are <u>confident</u> of a quick recovery.

Words ending *ance* and *ence*

In public speaking, <u>competence</u> and <u>experience</u> often make a big <u>difference</u> in engaging the <u>audience</u>. There's also plenty of <u>evidence</u> that a speaker's hard work and <u>patience</u> in preparing the talk increases their self-<u>confidence</u>.

C6 Verb Beginnings *a, co, su*

First Syllables before a double consonant letter: *a; co; su*

▶ Earworm

Collect, co**nnect** and co**rrect**
A**rrive**, a**pprove** and a**ffect**
A**ttract**, a**rrange** and a**pply**
Su**ggest**, su**pport** and **supply**

Verbs beginning with *a, co* and *su*

The consonant which comes after the verb beginnings *a, co* and *su* is usually spelt with a doubled letter, for example 'tt' in attract or 'rr' in *arrange*. These verb beginnings are generally unstressed, with the 'a', 'o' and 'u' pronounced as the reduced vowel sound /ə/. But note that there are exceptions, where the first syllable is stressed, for example, *access, suffer, correlate*.

Note: Some words with these beginnings are both verbs and nouns, but the pronunciation for most is the same, for example *account, attack, supply, support*.

Note: The explanation for consonant doubling in these words is historical: these consonant beginnings were originally the latin prefixes *ad* (to), *sub* (under) and *con* (with), but the final consonants of the prefixes changed to match the consonant at the start of the following syllable, for example *arrange* instead of *adrange, support* instead of *subport* and *collect* instead of *conlect*. This change results from a process known as assimilation.

Word recognition difficulty

Listeners need to be familiar with these very common syllables – they are easily missed. Learners may hear the stressed syllable as being the beginning of the word and this can lead to mistakes such as hearing *prove* instead of *approve*.

Raise awareness

Show learners the earworm and read it out for them [or ▶ play audio C6]. Read out the text line by line, inviting them to repeat keeping the same rhythm. Try to use the weak vowel /ə/ in the first syllable of all of the verbs, no matter how they are spelt.

Match beginnings and endings

Match the beginnings and endings to make verbs. Use each beginning three times. Then practice saying the verbs with the stress on the ending.

Beginnings: *a*; *co*; *su*

Endings: *LLOW; LLECT; PPLY; FFORD; PPOSE; RRIVE; RRECT; RRANGE; GGEST; PPORT; NNECT; MMAND*

> (**Answers:** *allow, apply, arrive, arrange, afford, collect, correct, connect, command, supply, suppose, suggest, support*)

Guess the spelling

Read out some verbs which the learners are unlikely to know, which have *a*, *su* and *co* as the first syllable. Ask them to write them down. This may be difficult on account of the letters 'a', 'o' and 'u' all being pronounced the same. You could choose words from the following lists.

> *attest, apprise, affirm*
>
> *supplant, suppress, surround*
>
> *corrode, connive, collude*

▶ Do a listening exercise

Read out the following news report [or ▶ play audio] and ask learners to listen and spot the verb beginnings given (they are <u>underlined</u>). You could organize this activity in different ways:

- ask learners to count the number of times they hear each syllable
- raise a hand each time they hear a word with one of the four syllables
- do the activity in teams, first listening for words with the syllables and after, trying to remember as many of them as possible
- ask learners to listen and make notes. Then they summarise the story from their notes.

> A recent opinion poll <u>suggests</u> that few people <u>support</u> hospital parking charges. Fees particularly <u>affect</u> staff, with many nurses saying they can no longer <u>afford</u> to drive to work. Hospitals <u>appear</u> to use parking fees as a way of <u>collecting</u> extra cash, but as one nurse explained, 'I can't <u>arrange</u> any alternative. I have to <u>arrive</u> at 5am, and there are no buses at that time'.

C7 Verb Beginnings *be, de, re, pre*

Verbs beginning with consonants plus '*e*': *be, de, re, pre*

▶ **Earworm**

Be**gin**, be**come** and be**lieve**
Re**port**, re**quest** and re**ceive**
Pre**pare**, pre**sent** and pre**tend**
De**cide**, de**sign** and de**fend**

Verbs beginning with *be, de, re, pre*

In verbs with two syllables, the first tends to be unstressed. If the vowel letter in the unstressed syllables is '*e*', speakers pronounce it as a reduced vowel: usually /ɪ/, but /ə/ is also possible. Listeners need to be familiar with these very common syllables – they are easily missed and this can lead to mistakes such as hearing *leave* instead of *believe*.

Note: Some words with these beginnings are both verbs and nouns, and the stress pattern may be different. For example, *present* as a verb has the stress on the second syllable, but as a noun it has the stress on the first. Others have the same stress pattern for both verb and noun, for example *report*.

Note: The verb beginnings *be, de, re* and *pre* are not always unstressed. For example, in *prejudice*, the first syllable is stressed and has the vowel sound /e/.

Note: Bear in mind that the spellings *re, de* and *pre* may appear as part of a bigger syllable such as *reck* in *reckon*. This lesson does not deal with these.

Emphatic use of the prefixes *de, re, pre*

Sometimes *re, de* and *pre* are clearly separable prefixes added to a verb, for example *send* and *resend*. In these words, the vowel in the prefix is not reduced – it is the full vowel sound /iː/. The prefixes add an extra meaning to the verb:

re = *do again*, for example *re* + *send* = *resend* (send again).
de = *do the opposite*, for example *de* + *construct* = *deconstruct* (take apart)
pre = *do before*, for example *pre* + *heat* = *preheat* (make it hot before starting)
There are some minimal pairs:
recount (reduced first vowel) = narrate
re-count (full first vowel) = count again

Raise awareness

Show learners the earworm and read it out for them [or ▶ play audio C7]. Read out the text line by line, inviting them to repeat keeping the same rhythm. Try to include a weak vowel in the first syllable of all of the verbs.

Match beginnings and endings

Match the beginnings and endings to make verbs. Use each beginning twice. Then practice saying the verbs with the stress on the ending.

Beginnings: *re; be; de; pre*

Endings: *CIDE; PARE; LAX; GIN; PEAT; LIEVE; SCRIBE; FER*

> (**Answers:** *relax, repeat, begin, believe, decide, describe, prepare, prefer. Other possible words include prescribe, relieve, defer*)

Do a dictation

Read out some verbs which the learners are unlikely to know, which have *re, de* and *pre* as the first syllable. Ask them to write them down. You could choose words from the following lists.

> *rebuff, recant, redress, refute*
>
> *decamp, degrade, deface, detest*
>
> *presume, preclude, prescind*

▶ Do a listening exercise

Read out the following news report [or ▶ play audio] and ask learners to listen and spot the verb beginnings given (these are <u>underlined</u>). You could organize this activity in different ways:

- ask learners to count the number of times they hear each syllable
- raise a hand each time they hear a word with one of the four syllables
- do the activity in teams, first listening for words with the syllables and after, trying to remember as many of them as possible
- do a follow-up activity focusing on the meaning of the words – see the suggested example below.

    Work <u>begins</u> next week on the new M30 motorway. The project has been <u>delayed</u> by protesters, but police are <u>believed</u> to be <u>preparing</u> to <u>remove</u> them today. According to <u>developers</u>, the motorway has been <u>designed</u> to <u>reduce</u> traffic pollution on smaller roads, but critics <u>predict</u> it will only <u>result</u> in more car journeys.

Follow-up

Ask learners to complete the words:

1 starts = be… (***Answer:*** *gins*)

2 made late = de… ***Answer:*** *layed*)

3 thought = be… (***Answer:*** *lieved*)

4 getting ready = pre… (***Answer:*** *paring*)

5 move away = re… (***Answer:*** *move*)

6 people who build = de… (***Answer:*** *velopers*)

7 planned = de… (***Answer:*** *signed*)

8 make less = re… (***Answer:*** *duce*)

9 say that in the future = pre… (***Answer:*** *dict*)

10 be the cause of = re… (***Answer:*** *sult*)

C8 Verb Beginnings *con, en, in*

Verb beginnings with 'n' or 'm' after the vowel: *con; com; en; em; in; im*

▶ Earworm

Com**pare**, con**trast** and con**trol**
En**joy**, en**quire**, en**rol**
Com**plain**, con**firm** and con**fess**
In**vent**, im**prove** and im**press**

Verb beginnings *con, com, en, em, in, im*

In verbs with two syllables, the first tends to be unstressed with a reduced vowel. In the verb beginnings con and com, the 'o' is typically the sound /ə/. For in and im, the 'i' is typically /ɪ/. For en and em, the 'e' varies – /ɪ/ for some speakers and /ə/ for others. Notice that the choice of 'n' or 'm' in these syllables depends on the letter which follows: it is usually 'n', but 'm' when the following letter is 'b' or 'p'.

Note: Some words with these beginnings are both verbs and nouns, and the stress pattern may be different. For example, *contrast* as a verb has the stress on the second syllable, but as a noun it has the stress on the first. Others have the same stress pattern for both verb and noun, for example *concern*.

Note: the verb beginnings *con, com, en, em, in* and *im* are not always unstressed. Here are some exceptions: *contact, comfort, comment, injure, enter, envy, empty*.

Raise awareness

Show learners the earworm and read it out for them [or ▶ play audio C8]. Read out the text line by line, inviting them to repeat keeping the same rhythm. Alternatively, learners may 'play' the text using text-to-speech software such as is available in Microsoft Word, and practice saying it by themselves.

Match beginnings and endings

Match the beginnings and endings to make verbs. Use each beginning once. Then practice saying the verbs with the stress on the ending.

Beginnings: con; com; en; em; in; im

Endings: PLOY; PROVE; CREASE; TAIN; JOY; PARE

(**Answers:** *contain, compare, enjoy, employ, increase, improve*)

Guess the spelling

Read out some verbs which the learners are unlikely to know, which have *con*, *com*, *en*, *em*, *in* and *im* as the first syllable. Ask them to write them down. You could choose words from the following lists.

condole, convene, compel, comprise

enact, encrust, emboss, embark

incite, inhale, impair, impound

▶ Do a listening exercise

Read out the following news report [or ▶ play audio] and ask learners to listen and spot the verb beginnings given (these are underlined). You could organize this activity in different ways:

- ask learners to count the number of times they hear each verb beginning
- raise a hand each time they hear a word with one of the verb beginnings
- do the activity in teams, first listening for words with the syllables and after, trying to remember as many of them as possible
- do a follow-up activity focusing on the meaning of the words – see the suggested example below.

  A man has confessed to starting a fire in Ocean Park after losing control of a barbecue. Fire services were informed after neighbours complained of thick smoke in the area. 'From today, the council will enforce a ban on barbecues', a spokesperson said. 'We want people to continue to enjoy the good weather', She insisted, 'but remember: confine cooking to kitchens!'

Follow-up

Ask learners to complete the words:

1 a man has con… (*fessed*)

2 after losing con… (*trol*)

3 fire services were in… (*formed*)

4 after neighbours com… (*plained*)

5 the council will en… (*force*)

6 we want people to con… (*tinue*)

7 to en… (*joy*) the good weather

8 she in… (*sisted*)

9 remember: con… (*fine*) cooking to kitchens!

C9 Noun ending *ity*

The noun suffix *ity*

▶ Earworm

Punctuality

I **know** that punctu**al**ity
Is **not** my speci**al**ity
I **don't** have that a**bil**ity
It's **not** a possi**bil**ity
I'm **full** of crea**tiv**ity
I'm **good** at sensi**tiv**ity
But **got** to face re**al**ity
I'm **bad** at punctu**al**ity

Nouns ending with *ity*

When listeners hear the common noun ending *ity*, they can be very confident that it is the end of a word. The 'i' may be pronounced as /ə/ or /ɪ/, and the final 'y' is /ɪ/. The 't' may difficult to hear clearly. A lot of speakers soften a /t/ between vowels so that it sounds more like a /d/ or an /r/ (this is known as *flapped t*). This variation in pronunciation may be confusing for listeners who are not accustomed to it.

A very noticeable feature of the *ity* ending is that it affects the stress of the word. For example, compare popular and popularity. The stress in the second word has moved to the syllable before the suffix *ity*. This also means a change in vowel sound. In the first word, the 'a' is the reduced vowel /ə/; in the second word, it is the full vowel /æ/. Listeners can expect the suffix *ity* to come immediately after the stressed syllable in a word.

Note: The sequence of letters *ity* is not always a suffix. For example, it's not a suffix in *pity*.

Raise awareness

Show learners the earworm and read it out for them [or ▶ play audio C9] – [there is also a rap version available]. Read out the text line by line, inviting them to repeat keeping the same rhythm. Make sure that the stress is on the syllable before the *ity* ending. Ask a few questions to focus on the meaning of the poem, for example:

What are the author's good and bad points?

Are you like this author? Why/Why not?

Match beginnings and endings

Match the beginnings and endings to make nouns. Use each beginning once. Then practice saying the nouns with the stress on the vowel in bold.

Beginning: act, ab, person, cel, univ, opport, electr, auth, curi, simil

*Ending: **a**lity, **a**rity, **e**brity, **e**rsity, **i**city, **i**lity, **i**vity, **o**rity, **o**sity, **u**nity*

(**Answers:** *activity, ability, personality, celebrity, university, opportunity, electricity, authority, curiosity, similarity*)

Guess the spelling

When note-taking, listeners will often have to write down words they haven't heard before, guessing the spelling from the sound. To develop this skill, you could dictate some invented words such as the examples below. Then ask learners to compare their spellings with a partner.

clavity, anarosity, celoranity, tenerity

Look up expressions including nouns with *ity*

The expressions below consist of a noun with *ity* followed by another word which collocates with it. Choose one and ask learners if they know the meaning of it: *Do you know the meaning of 'reality TV'?* If they don't know or seem uncertain, ask them to check it online. This will involve them either being able to type the phrase or repeat it in a way which is recognisable. This is an indirect form of dictation, and involves learners being able to identify the word boundary in the phrases. Repeat the activity with several of the expressions.

reality TV, priority boarding, maternity leave, disability benefits, utility bills, mobility scooter, publicity stunt, electricity supply, university campus, celebrity status, community centre, fertility treatment, hospitality industry, infinity pool, minority rule, popularity contest, curiosity shop, variety show, opportunity cost, superiority complex

▶ Do a listening exercise

Read out the following news report [or ▶ play audio] and ask learners to listen and spot the word ending *ity* (these are underlined). You could organize this activity in different ways:

- ask learners to count the number of times they hear a word with this ending
- raise a hand each time they hear a word with the ending
- do the activity in teams, first listening for words with the ending and after, trying to remember as many of them as possible

A group of celebrities have started a trek around the country to raise money for charity. The group are asking for equality of opportunity for people with disabilities, and for better facilities at schools and universities. A spokesman for the group said, 'We hope that the publicity will help to raise awareness of the problems faced by an important minority of people in the country. We will work to the best of our ability to turn dreams into a reality.

Follow-up

Read out the following sentences. Ask learners to complete the final word and then answer the question.

1 Have you ever met a celeb… (***Answer:*** *rity*)

2 Have you been to uni… (***Answer:*** *versity*)

3 Have you ever done something for char… (***Answer:*** *ity*)

4 How would you describe your person… (***Answer:*** *ality*)

5 What's your favourite leisure act… (***Answer:*** *ivity*)

6 At your school, how could you improve the facil… (***Answer:*** *ities*)

7 How can we help people with disab… (***Answer:*** *ilities*)

8 What would you do if you had the oppor… (***Answer:*** *tunity*)

C10 Nouns ending *ation*

The noun ending *ation*

▶ **Earworm**

> Frustration
>
> **Sitt**ing at the **sta**tion
> A**noth**er cancel**la**tion
> **What's** the situ**a**tion?
> **Need** an expla**na**tion
> **Wait** for infor**ma**tion
> **No** communi**ca**tion

Nouns ending with *ation*

When a listener hears the suffix *ation*, they can be confident that it is probably the end of a word, and the word is a noun (although there may be another suffix after it such as *al*). The word stress is always on the first syllable of the suffix – the 'a', which is pronounced as the vowel sound /eɪ/. However, the second syllable of the suffix is not quite as clear and audible. The 'ti' letter pair is pronounced /ʃ/, which will be confusing for listeners who expect to hear a /t/. The vowel after this is the reduced vowel /ə/, and it may be reduced so much that you don't hear any vowel sound at all.

Note that the suffix *ation* affects the stress of the word. For example, compare *inform* and *information*. In the first word, the stress is on 'form', and the vowel is the full vowel sound /ɔ:/. However in the second word, the stress has moved to 'a', and the vowel sound in form has become the reduced vowel sound /ə/.

Raise awareness

Show learners the earworm and read it out for them [or ▶ play audio C10] – [there is also a blues version available]. Alternatively, learners may 'play' the text using text-to-speech software such as is available in Microsoft Word. Elicit a response from the learners to the situation in the poem, for example:

> *Where's the speaker?*
>
> *What's happened?*
>
> *Why does the speaker feel angry?*
>
> *What would YOU do if you were in this situation?*

Then read out the text line by line, inviting them to repeat keeping the same rhythm.

▶ Do a note-taking exercise

Read out phone messages such as the ones below [or ▶ play audio] and ask learners to make a note of the most important information. Note that learners don't need to know the meaning of words like *aspiration*, *carnation* or *ovation* since they are proper names in this context. Familiarity with the suffix *ation* will help them to guess the spelling.

First message: Hello, this is Kim Nation speaking, from the Aspiration Foundation. I'm just ringing to thank you for your invitation to the open day.

Second message: Hi, this is Jo here, from the Carnation Station florists on Coronation Road, just to say that your order is ready for collection whenever you're ready.

Third message: Hi, I'm speaking from the Ovation Health Centre, just to say we've had a cancellation on Monday, so we could fit you in for your vaccination on that day if you're interested. Please let us know as soon as possible.

Make nouns from verbs

Say some verbs that the learners already know and ask them call out the related nouns. It's probably easiest to begin with verbs ending *ate*, for example *educate* (education), *decorate* (decoration), *calculate* (calculation), *separate* (separation), *communicate* (communication), *celebrate* (celebration). Then you could move on to less obvious ones, for example *inform* (information), *explain* (explanation), *cancel* (cancellation), *invite* (invitation), *relax* (relaxation), *present* (presentation).

To make the activity more challenging and game-like, you could include some verbs which <u>don't</u> have a noun form with *ation*, such as the ones below. As you say the verbs, learners have to call out the noun version with *ation*, but remain silent if there isn't one.

   enjoy, agree, move, escape, watch, complain, wait, answer, stay

Finish the final word

Say sentences where the last word is one which learners a likely to know ending with ation. Only say the beginning of the last word and encourage learners to call out the completion. This matches the kind of mental prediction that listeners use. Here are some examples:

   1 I'd just like some infor… (***Answer:*** *mation*)

   2 We're going out for a birthday cele… (***Answer:*** *bration*)

   3 Which country in the world has the biggest popu… (***Answer:*** *lation*)

   4 I'm going to hospital for an ope… (***Answer:*** *ration*)

   5 We sat together and had an interesting conver… (***Answer:*** *sation*)

   6 The American word for holiday is va… (***Answer:*** *cation*)

▶ Do a listening exercise

Read out the following news report [or ▶ play audio] and ask learners to listen and spot the suffix *ation* (these are <u>underlined</u>). You could organize this activity in different ways:

- ask learners to count the number of times they hear a word with this ending
- raise a hand each time they hear a word with the ending
- do the activity in teams, first listening for words with the ending and after, trying to remember as many of them as possible

Polling <u>stations</u> have now closed following today's general election. It's calculated that around 40% of the <u>nation's population</u> turned out to vote. Ballot papers are now being counted at <u>locations</u> up and down the country, but there is no official <u>information</u> about the results yet. However, there are already <u>celebrations</u> outside the headquarters of the governing party and we expect some form of <u>communication</u> from there soon.

C11 Noun endings *ion* and *ian*

The noun endings *ion* and *ian*

▶ **Earworm**

Family Passions

Mickey's a mu**sic**ian
He **won** a compe**tit**ion
His **song** about the **oc**ean
Filled us with e**mot**ion

His **mamm**a's on a **miss**ion
Be**came** a poli**tic**ian
To **win** in the e**lec**tions
You **gott**a make co**nnec**tions

His **papp**a's got a **pass**ion
It **is**n't just a **fash**ion
Gotta stop po**llut**ion
There **must** be a so**lut**ion!

Nouns ending with *ion* and *ian*

The noun endings *ion* and *ian* are very common, but they are unstressed and can be difficult to identify for two reasons:

1. The consonant which comes before the 'i' may be pronounced in a way which is unexpected for listeners who are learning English. All of the underlined consonants in these words ('t', 'ss', 'c') are typically pronounced /ʃ/: *emotion*; *mission*; *politician*

2. The final *on* or *an* sound identical: either /ən/ or just the /n/ with no vowel at all.

A clue in the stress

Nouns with the endings *ion* and *ian* always have the stress on the syllable before the ending. This is a regular pattern which can help listeners identify this ending in the stream of speech. Expert listeners will know it is either the end of a word, or will be followed by a very common suffix such as *al* or *able*.

Raise awareness

Show learners the earworm and read it out for them [or ▶ play audio C11] – [there is also a rap version available]. Alternatively, learners may 'play' the text using text-to-speech software such as is available in Microsoft Word. Ask one or two questions to focus on the meaning of the poem, for example:

Do you think the people in this family get on well with each other?

Would you get on with them?

Guess the spelling

When note-taking, listeners will often have to write down words they haven't heard before, guessing the spelling from the sound. To develop this skill, you could dictate some invented words such as the examples below. Then ask learners to compare their spellings with a partner.

perition, flotion, samatician, tompression, cantician

▶ Do a listening exercise

Read out the following news report [or ▶ play audio] and ask learners to listen and spot the suffix ion (these are underlined). You could organize this activity in different ways:

- ask learners to count the number of times they hear a word with this ending
- raise a hand each time they hear a word with the ending
- do the activity in teams, first listening for words with the ending and after, trying to remember as many of them as possible
- ask learners to listen and make notes. Then they summarise the story from their notes.

  During a live discussion on a local radio station, suspicion arose regarding a connection between a local fiction writer and a recent crime. Action was taken and permission was given to arrest the individual for further investigation. Evidence was discovered, leading to the conclusion that the writer was probably involved in the crime.

C12 Noun ending *ture*

The suffix *ture*

▶ **Earworm**

Profile

I'm **bas**ically a **mix**ture
Open to ad**ven**ture
Curious in **na**ture
Very keen on **cul**ture
Love to hear a **lec**ture
Like a lot of **lite**rature
Maybe in the **fu**ture
I'll **learn** to paint a **pic**ture

Nouns ending with *ture*

The ending ture is very common but it is always unstressed and can be difficult to identify for two reasons:

1 The 't' followed by 'u' blends to become /ʧ/, which may be unexpected for listeners who are learning English.

2 The whole sequence 'ure' maybe nothing more than the weak vowel /ə/, or /əʳ/, depending on the accent. For this reason, it is not very audible. Also, it may sound very different from how the learner expects from the spelling, leading to incomprehension.

Note: There are a few exceptions. One example is *caricature*: although the last syllable is unstressed, the vowel is not weak. Note also the adjective *mature* – here the *ture* ending is stressed.

Lost middles

The ending *ture* is unstressed, and sometimes it comes after other unstressed syllables. When there's a string of three unstressed syllables together, for example *temperature* or *literature*, the first of them is often cut. In these examples, the 'e' of the second syllable is likely to be lost: **temprature*, **litrature*. This can confuse the learner listener.

Raise awareness

Show learners the earworm and read it out for them [or ▶ play audio C12] – [there is also a rap version available]. Alternatively, learners may 'play' the text using text-to-speech software such as is available in Microsoft Word. Elicit a response from the learners to the situation in the poem, for example:

What sort of person is the speaker?

Would you need to change any of the poem to make it true for you?

Find the hidden words

Give learners the list of 'hidden words' below.

Hidden words: *feature, gesture, lecture, mixture, picture, structure, texture*

Now read out sentences **1–7**. Explain that each sentence has one of the words in the list 'hidden' in it. For example, *picture* is hidden in Sentence **1**, because it's pronounced exactly the same as *picked your*. Ask learners to match the sentences with the hidden words.

1 Who picked your flowers?

2 Did you collect your parcel?

3 Who mixed your drink?

4 Did you text your parents?

5 Can you defeat your enemies?

6 Did you construct your website?

7 Did you suggest your idea?

(**Answers: 1** *picture,* **2** *lecture,* **3** *mixture,* **4** *texture,* **5** *feature,* **6** *structure,* **7** *gesture*)

Dictate expressions including nouns with ture

The expressions below consist of a noun with *ture* followed by another word which collocates with it. Choose a few of them for a dictation exercise. Say each expression twice and ask learners to write what they hear. This involves learners being able to identify the word boundary in the phrases. Repeat the activity with several of the expressions.

literature festival, nature trail, adventure holiday, lecture theatre, future tense, picture frame, culture pages, temperature rises, feature film

▶ Do a listening exercise

Read out the following report [or ▶ play audio] and ask learners to listen and spot the suffix *ture* (these are <u>underlined</u>). You could organize this activity in different ways:

- ask learners to count the number of times they hear a word with this ending
- raise a hand each time they hear a word with the ending
- do the activity in teams, first listening for words with the ending and after, trying to remember as many of them as possible

<u>Literature</u> and <u>culture</u> are often intertwined, with <u>features</u> of the natural world frequently portrayed in the <u>structure</u> of stories. <u>Gestures</u> and <u>pictures</u> can add depth to <u>lectures</u>, giving readers a visual representation of the <u>adventure</u> described. As we look to the <u>future</u>, we can appreciate the way <u>literature</u> reflects the <u>nature</u> of the world around us.

C13 Adjectives ending *able* and *ible*

Adjectives ending *able* and *ible*

. . . .

▶ **Earworm**

Good Review
They're **comfor**table and **dur**able
They're **lov**able, a**dor**able
Fashionable but **sen**sible
To **me** they're indi**spen**sable

Bad Review
They're **horr**ible, un**bear**able
Un**suit**able, un**wear**able
They're **terr**ible, un**us**able
The **price** is inex**cus**able

Adjectives ending *able* and *ible*

The common suffix *able* (and *ible*) consists of two very weak syllables at the end of a word. The first of these is the reduced vowel /ə/(schwa). The second consists of a schwa between the consonants /b/ and /l/, but very often the vowel is so weak that it disappears completely, leaving the /l/ as a 'syllabic consonant'. This means that *able* (and *ible*) is difficult to hear. This problem is compounded if the listener expects it to be pronounced fully, as in *able* or *table*. For example, if your learner thinks that *comfortable* sounds like *come for table*, they may not recognise the actual word *comfortable* when they hear it.

Lost middles

Note that in some *able* words such as *comfortable*, a syllable may be lost in the middle of the word. For example, it may sound like *comftable*, with the 'or' cut. Other examples include *vegetable*, *reasonable*, *preferable*, *fashionable*, and *miserable*. This adds to the mismatch between what the learner expects to hear and what they actually hear. You could use the limerick below to raise awareness of reduced syllables and lost middles.

I knew a young woman called Mabel
Who slept on the kitchen table
Made herself comfortable
Head on a vegetable
Never knew how she was able

Raise awareness

Show learners the earworm and read it out for them [or ▶ play audio C13]. Alternatively, learners may 'play' the text using text-to-speech software such as is available in Microsoft Word. Elicit a response from the learners to the situation in the poem, for example:

Where might you expect to see a text like this?

What product could it be reviewing?

Do you always read reviews before buying things?

Then read out the text line by line, inviting them to repeat keeping the same rhythm.

Guess the spelling

When note-taking, listeners will often have to write down words they haven't heard before, guessing the spelling from the sound. To develop this skill, you could dictate some invented words such as the examples in **A** below, or phrases such as those in **B** below. Then ask learners to compare their spellings with a partner.

A: *faitable, anonable, immortable, perrible, corrotable, fallanible*

B: *miserable weather, reasonable price, preferable result, vulnerable child*

▶ Do a listening exercise

Read out the following news report [or ▶ play audio] and ask learners to listen and spot the suffixes *able* and *ible* (these are underlined). You could organize this activity in different ways:

- ask learners to count the number of times they hear a word with this ending
- raise a hand each time they hear a word with the ending
- do the activity in teams, first listening for words with the ending and after, trying to remember as many of them as possible.

  It was a miserable day, impossible to imagine. But somehow, she managed to be sensible and flexible in the face of some terrible difficulties. It seems incredible now, but by a clever use of the available resources, she found a reasonable solution and came out of it all in a comfortable situation.

C14 Adjective endings *ious* and *ous*

The adjective endings *ious* and *ous*

▶ **Earworm**

> Delicious
> This **fam**ous young **cook** from Mau**rit**ius
> Was **anx**ious but **also** am**bit**ious
> His **house** is not **grac**ious
> His **kitch**en's not **spac**ious
> But **man**, are his **dish**es de**lic**ious!

Adjectives ending *ious* and *ous*

The endings ious, and ous are unstressed and can be difficult to identify for two reasons:

1 The consonant before the ending *ious*, typically 't', 'c' or 'x', blends together with the 'i' to create the sound /ʃ/, (e.g. *delicious*) which may be unexpected for many learners.

2 The three-letter combination '*ous*' is reduced to the weak ending /əs/, which may be unexpected, and also quite difficult to hear.

Note: some ous words may have lost middles, where a middle syllable is cut. Here are some examples: *generous, marvellous, poisonous, dangerous*

Raise awareness

Show learners the earworm, which has the form of a limerick, and read it out for them [or ▶ play audio C14]. Alternatively, learners may 'play' the text using text-to-speech software such as is available in Microsoft Word. Elicit a response from the learners to the situation in the poem, for example:

> *Do you think the cook is rich? Why / Why not?*

> *Is he a good cook? How do you know?*

Then read out the text line by line, inviting them to repeat keeping the same rhythm.

Spotting words with ous

Read out words which end with /əs/ such as the following:

> *jealous, atlas, famous, Christmas, generous, nervous, harmless, octopus, mountainous, circus, focus, marvellous*

PronPack: Word Recognition for Listeners

Notice that although all of the words end /əs/, it is not always spelt the same. As they listen, ask learners to raise their hands <u>only</u> when they hear a word ending with the spelling 'ous'.

Guess the spelling

When note-taking, listeners will often have to write down words they haven't heard before, guessing the spelling from the sound. To develop this skill, you could dictate some invented words such as the examples in **A** below, or phrases such as those in **B** below. Then ask learners to compare their spellings with a partner.

A: *complicious, placious, tabulous, ronxious*

B: *generous gift, marvellous evening, poisonous plant, dangerous road*

▶ Do a listening exercise

Read out the following news report [or ▶ play audio] and ask learners to listen and spot the word ending *ious* and *ous* (these are <u>underlined</u>). You could organize this activity in different ways:

- ask learners to count the number of times they hear a word with this ending
- raise a hand each time they hear a word with the ending
- do the activity in teams, first listening for words with the ending and after, trying to remember as many of them as possible
- ask learners to listen and make notes. Then they summarise the story from their notes.

The <u>famous</u> singer-songwriter was known for her <u>ambitious</u> nature and <u>fabulous</u> voice. However, she was also <u>superstitious</u> and <u>jealous</u>, making <u>ridiculous</u> demands backstage. Some people were <u>suspicious</u> about her songs too, thinking that she didn't write them herself. However her performances were always <u>gorgeous</u> and she had an <u>enormous</u> following of dedicated fans.

C15 Adjective endings *al* and *ile*

Adjectives ending with *al* and *ile*

▶ **Earworm**

> **My Friend**
> Loyal and informal
> Logical and normal
> Mobile, agile
> Juvenile and fragile

Adjectives ending with *al* or *ile*

The ending *al* is unstressed in English. The vowel sound is very weak and may disappear completely, so the syllable is quite hard to hear. Another difficulty for some learners is that they may have similar words in their first language, but with the *al* syllable stressed, for example *normal*.

The *ile* ending is also unstressed in English, but the pronunciation varies. For example, North American speakers typically reduce the vowel to a schwa, while British speakers have a full vowel sound – the second half of *hostile* sounds like *tile*, for example. The text below is a rhyme in the US but not in the UK:

> *People in the hostel*
> *Seemed a little hostile*

Word families

Many *al* and *ile* words can have various suffixes added to make families of words. For example:

> **nor**mal, nor**mal**ity, **nor**malize, normali**za**tion

> **mo**bile, mo**bil**ity, **mob**ilize, mobili**za**tion

Notice how the stress and pronunciation changes across words in the family.
Note: In the UK, the 'z' may be replaced by an 's' in the endings *ize* and *ization*.

Raise awareness

Show learners the earworm and read it out for them [or ▶ play audio C15]. Read out the text line by line, inviting them to repeat keeping the same rhythm. Point out to the learners that the adjectives in lines 3 and 4 may be pronounced in two ways (see above).

Ask a few questions to focus on the meaning of the poem, for example:

What are the friend's good and bad points?

Would you have this person as a friend?

Accent differences

Say some of the words below in your own accent and ask learners to repeat the word in the other accent. For example, if you say the word the UK way, learners say it the US way. Alternatively, write words from the list into the video search engine YouGlish. Learners listen to a few of them and decide if the speaker is saying the word in the US way or they UK way.

> *agile, docile, fertile, fragile, futile, mobile, hostile, missile, senile, tactile, versatile, textile, volatile, reptile, juvenile*

▶ Do a listening exercise

Read out the following news report [or ▶ play audio] and ask learners to listen and spot the word ending *ile* (these are <u>underlined</u>). You could organize this activity in different ways:

- ask learners to count the number of times they hear a word with this ending
- raise a hand each time they hear a word with the ending
- do the activity in teams, first listening for words with the ending and after, trying to remember as many of them as possible

  The <u>textile</u> industry requires <u>versatile</u> materials that are <u>agile</u> yet durable, especially when catering to <u>juvenile</u> wearers. <u>Fertile</u> ground for innovation in this industry is found in the development of <u>mobile</u> <u>textiles</u> that can withstand <u>hostile</u> environments, as <u>futile</u> attempts to create <u>fragile</u> garments will not suffice.

Complete the families

Read out one or two of the word families below and get the learners to repeat. Then read out the first word or two of a family and ask learners to try to complete the family.

1 personal, personality, personalize, personalization

2 national, nationality, nationalize, nationalization

3 normal, normality, normalize, normalization

4 neutral, neutrality, neutralize, neutralization

5 equal, equality, equalize, equalization

6 general, generality, generalize, generalization

7 actual, actuality, actualize, actualization

8 real, reality, realize, realization

C16 Noun endings like *ology* and *onomy*

Words for academic subjects ending with *y*

▶ **Earworm**

> Studies
> Chemistry, biology
> Dentistry, ecology
> Philosophy, astronomy
> Or study the economy
> Botany, zoology
> History and technology
> Geology and geography
> And how about photography?

Subjects of study ending with 'y'

Noun endings for academic subjects often have endings like *ogy*, *omy*, *raphy*, *ophy*, *any*, *istry* and *ory*. These words have the stress on the third syllable from the end, which mean that all of these words have a characteristic rhythm, ending with two unstressed syllables (with the exception of *history*, where the middle syllable is lost). This familiar pattern can help listeners to identify the words and their endings.

Raise awareness

Show learners the earworm and read it out for them [or ▶ play audio C16]. Read out the text line by line, inviting them to repeat keeping the same rhythm. Make sure that the stress is on the syllable before the *ic* ending. Ask a few questions to focus on the meaning of the poem, for example:

> *Which subjects do you find most interesting?*

> *Are there any of them you have never studied?*

Match beginnings and endings

Ask learners to match the beginnings and endings to make nouns. Use each beginning once. Then practice saying the nouns with the stress on the vowel in bold.

Beginning: e**col**, pho**tog**, **bot**, bi**ol**, **chem**, **hist**, **geog**, ge**ol**, phi**los**, tech**nol**, **dent**, as**tron**

Ending: any, istry, ogy, ogy, omy ophy ory, raphy

(**Answers:** *ecology, photography, botany, biology, chemistry, history, geography, geology, philosophy, technology, dentistry, astronomy*)

Predict names of academic subjects

Ask learners to guess the names of the academic subjects related to the words below. Ask them to say the words, remembering that the stress should be on the third syllable from the end.

climate, ocean, mineral, society, Egypt, forest, toxic, escape, crime, music, cinema, poem

(**Answers:** *clima**tol**ogy, ocea**nog**raphy, mine**ral**ogy, soci**ol**ogy, Egyp**tol**ogy, **for**estry, toxi**col**ogy, esca**pol**ogy, crimi**nol**ogy, musi**col**ogy, cinema**tog**raphy, **po**etry*)

Related words

Many subject words with endings like *ology* and *onomy* belong to families of related words, for example:

photograph, pho**tog**raphy, pho**tog**rapher, photo**graph**ic

e**con**omy, eco**nom**ics, e**con**omist, eco**nom**ic

Notice how the stress and pronunciation changes across words in the family.

Ask learners if they can think of any words which are related to the academic subjects in the earworm text.

(**Possible answers:** *chemist, chemical, biologist, biological, dentist, ecologist, ecological, philosopher, philosophical, astronomer, astronomical, botanist, botanical, zoologist, zoological, historian, historical, technician, technological, geologist, geological, geographer, geographical*)

▶ Do a listening exercise

Read out the following news report [or ▶ play audio] and ask learners to listen and spot the subjects of study (these are underlined). You could organize this activity in different ways:

- ask learners to count the number of times they hear a subject.
- raise a hand each time they hear a subject
- do the activity in teams, first listening for subjects and after, trying to remember as many of them as possible

Long ago, there was a scientist named Sophia who was passionate about chemistry and biology. She was also interested in geography and ecology. She believed that philosophy and economy were essential to understanding the world around us. She spent her life studying history and technology to make the world a better place.

C17 Adverb ending *ly*

Adverbs ending with *ly*

▶ **Earworm**

> Victory
>
> We're **hope**fully **prac**tically **done**
> It **was**n't par**tic**ularly **fun**
> Let's **call** it a **day**
> We can **prob**ably **say**
> We've **bas**ically **act**ually **won**!

Adverbs ending with *ly*

The word ending *ly* is very common since most adverbs have this suffix. On it's own, it isn't necessarily problematic for listeners, but together with other suffixes such as *al*, *ful* or *able*, it can create difficult strings of unstressed syllables, and speakers sometimes cut syllables completely (see **B11** 'Lost Middles'). Here are some examples:

> *hopefully* – sounds like **hopefly*
> *practically* – sounds like **practicly*
> *particularly* – sounds like **particuly*
> *probably* – sounds like **probly*
> *basically* – sounds like **basicly*
> *actually* – sounds like **actuly*

Raise awareness

Show learners the earworm and read it out for them [or ▶ play audio C17]. Read out the text line by line, inviting them to repeat keeping the same rhythm. Point out to the learners that the adverbs (ending in *ly*) may be simplified (see above). Ask a few questions to focus on the meaning of the poem, for example:

> *What do you think the people were doing?*

> *What have they won?*

▶ Listen to adverbs in context

Ask learners to type in some of the adverbs from the earworm into a video search engine like YouGlish and decide how many of the examples have a syllable cut. For example, the word *practically* pronounced carefully would have four syllables. Ask learners to decide how many of the examples on YouGlish have only three syllables – more than half? Less than half?

Say it to hear it

It isn't necessary for learners to cut syllables in adverbs in their own speech – in fact, careful pronunciation is likely to be more intelligible. However, trying to say the reduced forms of these words can help them to fix this sound pattern in mind so that they will be more receptive to it as listeners. For this purpose, you can use the earworm as a kind of drill for the learners to practice saying the adverbs. You can also use the sentence-building drills below, where the sentences get progressively longer as you add adverbs. Learners repeat each line after you [or ▶ use audio].

It's nice.
It's awfully nice.
It's usually awfully nice.
Thankfully, it's usually awfully nice.

It's ruined.
It's totally ruined.
It's basically totally ruined.
Unfortunately, it's basically totally ruined.

I'm not bothered.
I'm not particularly bothered.
I'm actually not particularly bothered.
Honestly, I'm actually not particularly bothered.

▶ Do a listening exercise

Read out the following story [or ▶ play audio] and ask learners to listen and spot the adverbs (these are underlined). You could organize this activity in different ways:

- ask learners to count the number of times they hear an adverb.
- raise a hand each time they hear an adverb
- do the activity in teams, first listening for adverbs and after, trying to remember as many of them as possible.

At three o'clock, Derek was still stuck on the train. Now it would be practically impossible for him to reach the airport on time. He really didn't want to miss his flight, particularly as he had to make it to an important meeting. If he missed the plane, the whole trip would basically be pointless. Fortunately he didn't have any bags to check in, so hopefully he would be able to reach the boarding gate quickly. But in the end, he probably needn't have worried because the plane was actually delayed by three hours!

Follow up questions:

What would be practically impossible?
Why didn't Derek want to miss the plane?
What helped him reach the boarding gate quickly?
Why was there no need to worry in the end?

C18 Place name endings like *ton* and *ham*

Common place name endings in English

▶ **Earworm**

People and Places

Rutherford and Redford
Never went to Bedford
Merton, Burton?
Never knew for certain
Tottenham and Rotherham?
Didn't want to bother 'em
Edinburgh, Scarborough
There I met Barbara
Leicester, Gloucester
That's where I lost 'er

Place name endings like *ton* and *ham*

Through frequent use by local people, the pronunciation of place names has often moved far away from spelling. This is usually to make the name easier to say by reducing the vowels and cutting consonants, or sometimes whole syllables. This can be problematic for listeners who are familiar with the written form of the names. Many of these place names are also names of people or businesses such as football clubs.

Learners can't be expected to know the pronunciation of all names, but there are some very common endings which it's worth being aware of. These include

ton, ford, burgh or borough, bury, ham, cester

The vowel sound is reduced to schwa in most of these. In the case of *borough*, there are two schwa sounds in the ending, and the first of them is often cut, and the 'gh' is silent. In *bury*, the first vowel is often cut. In *ford* and *ham*, the 'r', 'h' are often cut. In the case of *cester*, the first syllable is cut so that it sounds like *ster*, and the final 'r' may also be cut.

Here are some examples. The upside-down e symbol represents the schwa sound.

Tottenham = *Totnəm

Leicester = *Leistə

Oxford = *Oxfəd

Glastonbury = *Glastonbry

Edinburgh = *Edimbərə

Kingston = *Kingstən

Accent variation

Names with these endings are not always pronounced the same. For example, in towns like *Birmingham*, the 'h' in *ham* is often pronounced by US speakers but not by UK speakers. The last vowel in Edinburgh is often pronounced as a full vowel /əʊ/ by US speakers. US speakers may not cut the first vowel in bury.

Raise awareness

Show learners the earworm and read it out for them [or ▶ play audio C18] – [there is also a rap version available]. Read out the rhyme line by line, inviting them to repeat keeping the same rhythm.

▶ Do a listening exercise

Read out the following news report [or ▶ play audio] and ask learners to listen and spot the names (these are underlined). You could organize this activity in different ways:

- ask learners to count the number of times they hear a name with one of the endings in this lesson.
- raise a hand each time they hear a name
- do the activity in teams, first listening for names and after, trying to remember as many of them as possible

Celia Clifford took the underground from Leicester Square to Euston and then took a train for Birmingham. During the journey, she watched animal documentaries by David Attenborough on her tablet. She got so involved that she didn't notice any of the stations they passed though – Northampton and Nottingham, then Castleford, Darlington and Durham, and next thing she know, she was in Edinburgh. She'd got on the train to Scotland by mistake!

Section D Resources

This section includes supplementary resources and materials including the PronPack Sound Chart and a glossary of terms.

- Reference chart of phonemic symbols and infographic
- Glossary of terms
- Bibliography
- About the Author
- Acknowledgements
- The PronPack Collection

Note: Printable / projectable Sound Charts in this section can be downloaded from the Resources section for PronPack: Connected Speech for Listeners on the accompanying website at PronPack.com as well as worksheets and audio for lessons in **sections B** and **C**. Videos are also available for many of the activities.

D1 PronPack Sound Chart

IPA Phonemic Symbols with Guide Words

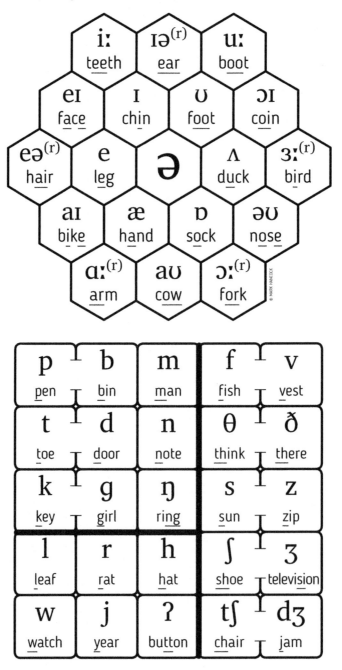

p pen	b bin	m man	f fish	v vest
t toe	d door	n note	θ think	ð there
k key	g girl	ŋ ring	s sun	z zip
l leaf	r rat	h hat	ʃ shoe	ʒ television
w watch	j year	ʔ button	tʃ chair	dʒ jam

acoustic memory: memory of the way something sounds

assimilation: when two consonants are next to each other in connected speech, and one of them changes in some way, becoming more like the other

authentic: material used in ELT which was not specifically created for teaching purposes – it is natural, rather than artificial

blending: where neighbouring sounds mix together in connected speech – also called fusion or coalescence

citation form: the typical sound of a word when said on its own, as an example of how it should be pronounced. Also called dictionary pronunciation

coda: the part of a syllable which comes after the vowel sound

consonant cluster: two or more consonant sounds next to one another in a word or phrase

content word: words such as nouns, verbs and adjectives, which are meaningful independently of the grammar of a sentence. Not function words.

contraction: where two words blend together. Shown in writing with an apostrophe, for example I'm for I am.

corpus: a collection of texts being used as a source of examples of language in use

d-drop: Richard Cauldwell's term for elision of /d/

decoding: the process of identifying words in the sound of continuous speech

dictionary pronunciation: the typical sound of a word when said on its own, as an example of how it should be pronounced. Also called citation form

earworm: a short text which is memorable, usually because it contains an element of wordplay such as rhyme, rhythm or alliteration

EFL: English as a foreign language

ELF: English as a Lingua Franca

elision: when one or more sounds are cut from words in connected speech

ELT: English language teaching

ESL: English as a second language

exemplar view: the idea that words are stored in the memory in all the forms we have heard, rather than in one perfect citation form

familiarity effect: the idea that speakers are more likely to reduce the vowels in words they use frequently

folk phonetics: any informal way of writing the pronunciation words and phrases

function word: words such as prepositions, pronouns and auxiliary verbs, which are used to show grammar rather than to refer to specific things; not content words

fusion: when two neighbouring sounds mix together to create another sound, also called blending or coalescence

gap fill: a learning exercise type which involves putting words or phrases in gaps

glottal stop: a brief silence made by closing the glottis to stop the airstream in the throat

homophone: two different words which sound exactly the same

hyper-articulation: when speakers deliberately pronounce words more clearly than normal

IPA: the symbols of the international phonetic alphabet used to represent pronunciation

lexical segmentation: the process by which we are able to divide the stream of speech into separate words

linking: the way one word joins the next in connected speech

lost middles: unstressed syllables in the middles of words which are often cut

non-rhotic: accents in which the /r/ is not pronounced unless there is a vowel sound after it

onset: the part of a syllable which comes before the vowel sound

peak: the vowel sound which forms the central part, and sometimes the only part, of a syllable

phonological form: the form of a word as it is pronounced rather than as it is written

phrasal homophone: two different phrases which sound exactly the same

pop spelling: a way of spelling a word or phrase as it sounds, often used in informal texts such as pop lyrics

productive: the skills of writing and speaking, which involve producing something

receptive: the skills of reading and listening, which involve perceiving something

rhotic: accents in which the /r/ is pronounced, even where there is no vowel sound after it

schwa: the neutral, reduced vowel sound which is found in many unstressed syllables in varieties of English such as British and American

spelling pronunciation: pronouncing a word as it appears from the spelling, rather than as it is normally pronounced by speakers of the language

spoken word recognition: the skill of identifying words in their spoken form in natural speech

squeeze zones: a term introduced by Richard Cauldwell to refer to areas of an utterance where there are two or more unstressed syllables next to each other

stress deaf: inability to perceive stress caused by the fact that stress is not used meaningfully in the speakers' first language

stress: the way some syllables are made to stand out, by being longer, louder or marked by a change of pitch

stress-neutral: suffixes which have no effect on the word stress in the root word

stress-shifting: suffixes which cause a change of position in the word stress of the root word

syllabic consonant: a consonant, usually /l/ or /n/, which can function as a syllable even when there is no vowel sound present

trictation: a dictation-type activity for which there is more than one correct answer

unvoiced: speech sounds which don't involve vibration of the vocal cords

voiced: speech sounds which involve vibration of the vocal cords

vowel reduction: making vowels shorter and easier to say, for example replacing the original vowel sound with a schwa

weak form: the form of a function word which occurs in connected speech, when it has a reduced vowel and sometimes elision of one of its phonemes

working memory: a temporary memory used in the immediate process of listening but then forgotten

D3 Bibliography

Brown, A. (2018). ***Understanding and Teaching English Spelling.*** Routledge

Cauldwell, R. (2018). ***A Syllabus for Listening – Decoding.*** Speech in Action

Cutler, A. (2012). ***Native Listening : Language Experience and the Recognition of Spoken Words.*** MIT Press

Field, J. (2008). ***Listening in the Language Classroom.*** Cambridge University Press

Hancock, M. & McDonald, A. (2014). ***Authentic Listening Resource Pack.*** Delta Publishing

Hancock, M. (2017). ***PronPack 3: Pronunciation Pairworks.*** Hancock McDonald ELT

Jones, Roach, Setter & Esling, (2011). ***The Cambridge English Pronouncing Dictionary.*** Cambridge University Press

D4 About the Author

Mark Hancock is a well-known ELT author, teacher and trainer with over 30 years experience in the field. He has taught in Sudan, Turkey, Brazil, Spain and the UK.

Pronunciation has been a special interest for much of his career and he has written several popular, award-winning textbooks on the topic. Mark regularly presents on teacher training courses and at international events, both online and face to face.

In his free time Mark is a keen artist and musician, playing guitar and saxophone. He also enjoys walking in the mountains.

Books by the same author

PronPack: Connected Speech for listeners (Hancock McDonald ELT, 2022)

Mark Hancock's 50 Tips for Teaching Pronunciation (CUP, 2020)

PronPack 1-6 (Hancock McDonald ELT, 2017-2021)

Empower C1 'Everyday English' sections (CUP, 2016)

Oxford Advanced Learner's Dictionary 9th Ed 'Speaking Tutor' section (OUP, 2015)

Authentic Listening Resource Pack (Delta, 2014 – co-authored with Annie McDonald)

English Pronunciation in Use Intermediate (CUP, 2003, 2012)

English Result (OUP, 2007-2010 – co-authored with Annie McDonald)

Pen Pictures 1-3 (OUP, 1999-2000 – co-authored with Annie McDonald)

Singing Grammar (CUP, 1999)

Pronunciation Games (CUP, 1995)

D5 Acknowledgements

My first book **Pronunciation Games** was published in 1995 by Cambridge University Press and designed by my sister Amanda Hancock. I would like to thank her for collaborating once again all these years later. I suspect the fact that **PronPack 1-4** were awarded the ELTons prize for Innovation in Teacher Resources was largely a result of her contribution. This book is a continuation of that same **PronPack** project.

A special thank you also to my partner Annie McDonald, whose part in this was in no way limited to her editorial help. Both of us share a long-standing special interest in ELT listening skills, and this led to our co-authored book **Authentic Listening Resource Pack** (Delta, 2014). Annie has been heavily involved in the development of the **Pronunciation for Listening** series right from the very start, from the broad idea right down to the fine detail.

Of the authors listed in the bibliography, I should make special mention of John Field. I have drawn on his work extensively for the ideas in this book.

D6 About PronPack

PronPack is an award-winning collection of resource books to help teachers focus on English pronunciation in class

Visit PronPack.com for information about the printed books and ebooks in the PronPack Collection which include:

PronPack 1: Pronunciation Workouts
Print ISBN: 9780995757516
eBook ISBN: 9780995757554

PronPack 2: Pronunciation Puzzles
Print ISBN: 9780995757523
eBook ISBN: 9780995757561

PronPack 3: Pronunciation Pairworks
Print ISBN: 9780995757530
eBook ISBN: 9780995757578

PronPack 4: Pronunciation Poems
Print ISBN: 9780995757547
eBook ISBN: 9780995757585

PronPack 5: Pronunciation of English for Spanish speakers
Print ISBN: 9780995757509
eBook ISBN: 9780995757592

PronPack 6: Pronunciation of English for Brazilian learners
Print ISBN: 9781838404000
eBook ISBN: 9781838404017

PronPack: Connected Speech for listeners
Print ISBN: 9781838404024
eBook ISBN: 9781838404031

PronPack: Word Recognition for listeners
Print ISBN: 9781838404048
eBook ISBN: 9781838404055

Printed in Great Britain
by Amazon

28647832R00066